Taming Childhood?

Rob Creasy · Fiona Corby

Taming Childhood?

A Critical Perspective on Policy, Practice and Parenting

Rob Creasy
School of Psychological and Social Sciences
York St John University
York, UK

Fiona Corby
School of Social Sciences, Humanities and Law
Teesside University
Middlesbrough, UK

ISBN 978-3-030-11841-9   ISBN 978-3-030-11842-6 (eBook)
https://doi.org/10.1007/978-3-030-11842-6

Library of Congress Control Number: 2018968337

© The Editor(s) (if applicable) and The Author(s) 2019
This work is subject to copyright. All rights are solely and exclusively licensed by the Publisher, whether the whole or part of the material is concerned, specifically the rights of translation, reprinting, reuse of illustrations, recitation, broadcasting, reproduction on microfilms or in any other physical way, and transmission or information storage and retrieval, electronic adaptation, computer software, or by similar or dissimilar methodology now known or hereafter developed.
The use of general descriptive names, registered names, trademarks, service marks, etc. in this publication does not imply, even in the absence of a specific statement, that such names are exempt from the relevant protective laws and regulations and therefore free for general use.
The publisher, the authors and the editors are safe to assume that the advice and information in this book are believed to be true and accurate at the date of publication. Neither the publisher nor the authors or the editors give a warranty, express or implied, with respect to the material contained herein or for any errors or omissions that may have been made. The publisher remains neutral with regard to jurisdictional claims in published maps and institutional affiliations.

Cover illustration: © Melisa Hasan

This Palgrave Pivot imprint is published by the registered company Springer Nature Switzerland AG
The registered company address is: Gewerbestrasse 11, 6330 Cham, Switzerland

To all the tame children who should be climbing trees, riding bikes, and taking risks. And to our own children, Leanne, Tom & Eddie who have been out there in the world, untamed having adventures. Yes, it was scary at times.

Preface

Not long after The Taming of Education had been completed, we were walking through Clumber Park in Nottinghamshire when a youngster of about 5 came towards us on a bike. What stood out was although this was a path in a park, the young cyclist was wearing a helmet, knee pads, and gloves, and mum was close behind constantly shouting instructions. Here was a child who wasn't being given any space. We had already had numerous discussions about children and parenting and how the notion of taming fit as a way of understanding just what is happening with regard to children's lives and this cyclist was the catalyst. Children are being increasingly tamed.

We seem to have written Taming Childhood at a pertinent time. Other commentators are drawing attention to the ways in which children are being subject to what we call taming. This is epitomised by the pejorative term, snowflake. After childhood has been tamed, young people are then subject to criticism for not being able to cope with what we have never allowed them to be exposed to. This book explores how this situation has come to be.

York, UK   Rob Creasy
Middlesbrough, UK   Fiona Corby

Contents

1 Introduction   1
   1.1 Introduction   1
   1.2 Structure of the Book   6
   References   10

2 The Context of Childhood   13
   2.1 Introduction   14
   2.2 The Individual Child: Neoliberalism to New Labour   15
   2.3 Children as Beings or Becomings   17
   2.4 Well-Being and Well-Becoming   21
   2.5 Vulnerability   25
   2.6 Resilience   27
   References   30

3 Introducing Tameness   35
   3.1 Introduction   36
   3.2 Snowflakes   38
   3.3 Conceptualising Issues as Wicked or Tame   41

3.4	From Paradigms to Evidence-Based Practice	44
3.5	The 10 Properties of Wicked Problems	47
3.6	Wickedity as a Continuum	49
3.7	Conclusion: The Possibility of Childhood	51
References		53

4 Home and Family — 57
4.1	Introduction	58
4.2	Parents and the Place of Children	60
4.3	Helicopter Parents	64
4.4	Parental Surveillance	68
4.5	Not Going Out	69
4.6	Children in a Changing Landscape	71
4.7	Conclusion	76
References		76

5 Taming in the Early Years — 83
5.1	Introduction	84
5.2	The Growing Role of the State	86
5.3	Towards Education	90
5.4	Readiness for School, or to Work?	92
5.5	Protecting the Early Years	94
5.6	Conclusion	96
References		98

6 Tameness at School — 103
6.1	Introduction	104
6.2	School Spaces	105
6.3	Starting School, Meeting Targets, Becoming Data	108
6.4	Metrics and the Datafication of Children	110
6.5	Making School Uniform	114
6.6	Conclusion: The Purpose of School	118
References		120

7	**Conclusion**	125
	7.1 Introduction	126
	7.2 What's Best for Children?	129
	7.3 Resisting Tameness	132
	References	136

References	137
Index	157

1

Introduction

Abstract In recent decades, UK society has seen a number of changes which increase pressure on children. This has contributed to the reported deterioration in the **mental health** of children alongside an increasing level of **unhappiness**. It appears as though children and young people lack **resilience**. Taming **Childhood** presents an argument regarding how social changes are contributing to children experiencing life in ways that are increasingly restricted and impoverished, what we refer to as tame. We argue that this is not a positive development, it is a childhood which restricts what children can do, undermining the development of resilience and undermining well-being.

Keywords Mental health · Unhappiness · Resilience · Childhood

1.1 Introduction

This book considers a range of factors which may be seen as influencing the context of childhood within the UK, putting forward the argument that childhood has changed in ways which are not in the best interests of either children or society. It adapts the concept of wicked and tame as first introduced by Rittel and Webber (1973) and presents this as an evaluative tool with which we might view childhood. In doing so, it develops an argument that the changing nature of childhood is having a negative impact upon children and young people's ability to achieve well-being within contemporary UK society.

For example, The Children's Society (2018) notes that since 2010 children are reporting less happiness with their lives, especially amongst children facing multiple disadvantages. Action for Children reports that 1 in 3 13- to 15-year-old children has mental health problems (2018) attributing this to a range of social factors. Similarly, the Mental Health Foundation (2016) indicates that mental health amongst children and young people is deteriorating. This is supported by the Care Quality Commission (2017) which indicate that the numbers of children and young people seeking help from mental health services have been rising over a number of years.

Some degree of caution may be appropriate in considering this rise. Sociologists have put forward arguments relating to how aspects of life may come to be redefined as medical concerns for some time. This medicalisation of life may result in an apparent increase in mental health problems as a consequence of changes in ways of understanding or categorising rather than in terms of actual, or real, changes. This may be identified, for example, within the growth of a therapeutic culture that is discussed later. However, the problems that reports, such as the ones referred to above, document regarding the significant growth in respect of the numbers of children and young people presenting with mental health problems cannot be dismissed as unfounded, as this issue does frame childhood today.

For Palmer (2009, 2015), UK society is toxic. James (2009) is more explicit and claims that life in Britain is making children mentally ill. We do not consider that there is any one reason for this, nor are the reasons simple. Instead, we point to the ways in which the lived world of children within the UK, what we might refer to as childhood, is shaped by policies, professional practices, and parenting in ways which are increasingly impoverishing childhood. In a society which seems preoccupied with well-being, we seem to be undermining the well-being of children.

When considering a broader picture of well-being, a number of accounts provide evidence which demonstrates that children in the UK fare poorly when compared to other countries (Aynsley-Green 2018; OECD 2009; Bradshaw et al. 2007). This is often presented as being a consequence of key measurements for material deprivation, poor health or low educational outcomes. The argument that we put forward here is concerned with the way in which the child's lived world increasingly provides fewer opportunities within which to develop and maintain resilience. In turn, we are arguing that well-being is supported by resilience. As such, a lack of resilience will therefore undermine well-being.

In making such a claim, we are working from the premise that there will always be pressures upon children. We recognise also that childhood is not universal, that some children will experience more pressures and some will experience fewer. Importantly, all children will experience some pressures which it is not possible to classify in this context as being any worse or better than others. At the same time, in focusing upon childhood within the UK, we are arguing that there have been a number of social developments over time which have increased the pressure on children. For example, we can see this in the intensification of education through an ever-increasing emphasis upon educational testing and examination results as is typified by the introduction of SATs in 1991 reinforced by OFSTED and League tables.

The example of SATs can be said to be one of example of a change which has widespread influence across society. In a similar vein, it can be argued that responsibility for children has become firmly located within families and with parents (Vincent 2017). The idea that it takes a village to raise a child is something that seems to have ceased to have meaning within contemporary UK society with a corresponding intensification of focus on the role of parents. At the same time, the experiences of children and families tend to be viewed in a manner which removes any consideration of their social or economic context such as experiencing poverty or facing adversity.

What will be considered throughout the book is that as UK society has changed in ways which increase the pressure upon children, including developments such as changes to parenting styles or the heightened sense of risk that permeates contemporary society, this can be seen to have led to a changed experience for children. It is the combination of a number of changes which have had a cumulative effect of reducing opportunities for the development of resilience by restricting what children are allowed to do or where they are permitted to go.

In relation to concerns about children, in recent years, the idea of well-being has become increasingly prevalent (Children's Society 2018; Bradshaw 2016; Taylor 2011; Ben-Arieh 2006; Sointu 2005). Alongside the concern with well-being though, especially with respect to childhood, is the associated concept of well-becoming. In fact, it may be fair to say that our actual concern with well-being is well-becoming. A major factor in the increasing levels of concern with children and their childhoods is the activity of UNICEF in reporting on childhood across the globe, especially in relation to the United Nations Convention on the Rights of the Child (UNCRC), (UNICEF 1989). It is perhaps noticeable that concerns with well-being have arisen in a period when there has been a growing realisation that the social context of childhood, the child's lived world, may often be having a negative impact upon the child.

Our concern here then is with the lived world of the child. We argue that in the UK, children's experiences are being stifled. The stifling that we refer to is not the consequence of one particular change or development, nor is it carried out with that purpose in mind. In many ways, the stifling of children's experiences is wrapped up in ideas about what is best for children, or what it means to be a good parent. What will be demonstrated then is that there is a complexity to the experience of childhood and that it is subject to a number of competing discourses. To provide a way of appreciating how different factors impact upon childhood, we adopt the lexicon provided by Rittel and Webber (1973) as will be explored further in Chapter 3, and argue that childhood is becoming increasingly tame; importantly though we assert that this is not in the child's best interests.

The basis of the argument offered by Rittel and Webber (1973) is that society is often faced by problems, but whereas some problems can be addressed by logical or structured approaches, approaches which will consistently work as a consequence of the nature of the problem, other problems are resistant to such solutions. This leads to the distinction being drawn between problems which are tame, which follow certain patterns, and those which are wicked as a consequence of their complexity and the way in which a solution that may usually work will not work in all situations.

Instead of focusing on problems, as Rittel and Webber do, we consider the lived world as it is constituted by policy and practice. In using the term practice though we encompass both the practice of practitioners, and the practice of parents. Policy and practice can often be seen as seeking simplistic solutions to complex problems and following from this, we argue that tameness is associated with control. In general, though the aims of control are to ensure predictability and/or consistency. A tame childhood is a childhood wherein both spontaneity and the child's capacity to employ agency and to self-direct are reduced.

It is worth noting then, at this point, that we are not concerned with socialisation. Socialisation can be explained as the developing, or inculcating of the skills and capacities that are required to operate within any given culture and is a key feature of traditional sociological concerns about children. As part of this, socialisation is concerned with how children learn to behave. Taming goes beyond this, in that it is concerned with the social context in which childhood is experienced. Our argument is that actions which can be seen as taming childhood have the effect of reducing and impoverishing the child's lived world. In this book, we argue that wickedity and, especially, tameness can be used as an evaluative lens through which to understand social developments. These concepts will be explained fully in Chapter 3. Tameness is presented as being against the best interests of children in the long term and ignores the complexity of children's social experience. A tame childhood is unlikely to provide opportunities for personal growth or for the development and maintenance of resilience. Where Rittel and Webber provide the basis of the concept of tameness, we will also draw upon other theoretical approaches to explain more general social issues such as the way in which the power of the State shapes individuals in ways which result in docility, or the value of understanding how competing discourses influence policy and practice.

For example, in spite of differing theoretical approaches towards understanding childhood, for practitioners and parents, there is much to suggest that the empirical differences between children and adults, such as physical size and appearance, along with intellectual ability underpin the viewing of children through a deficit model. This lends support to seeing them primarily in terms of their future selves. This can be seen in the ways in which the relationship between childhood and education is often viewed from the perspective of human capital theory wherein education is reduced to the position of an investment (Hartog and Oosterbeek 2007). We do recognise that in academic circles, there has been a move towards seeing children as beings, rather than becomings, but consider that such a position is not necessarily shared by parents, practitioners or policy-makers. For parents and practitioners, the discourse of children as becomings still remains highly influential, though that is not to say that they are necessarily conscious of this.

Importantly, the primacy of seeing children as becomings has the tendency to ignore their agency in the here and now and undermines their viewpoint and knowledge. Children may be physically weaker than adults, and they may think differently or not have as much knowledge, but it is the greater power that adults possess which is then used against children because of their weakness. In turn, it is the power possessed by adults which contributes to the vulnerability of children. In turn, this legitimises efforts to shape the future for children and has contributed to both policy-makers and practitioners assuming responsibility for this. This is not only the consequence of purposeful actions. Discourses about risk and parenting also contribute to the ways in which childhood is becoming increasingly tame.

1.2 Structure of the Book

Structuring a book always involves making decisions which can be contested. We have sought to impose a structure which makes sense, but we acknowledge that the five substantial chapters which form the basis of the book inevitably throw up issues and examples which are not exclusive to each chapter. There are parts of the book where the chapters may be seen as overlapping to a greater or lesser degree. If we take

Chapters 4–6 in particular, we could see how home, family, early years, and school cannot be rigidly divided to the extent that each is dealt with in isolation. Importantly though, this book is concerned with aspects of social life and social life does not lend itself to such a tame structure. In dealing with each issue separately, this has been done to facilitate access to our overall argument.

We could therefore have incorporated the concepts that are covered in Chapter 2 in later chapters as they apply to a range of issues which arise in families, in the early years, and in school. We felt that this would provide less clarity and so determined to set out these key concepts from the outset. In doing so, Chapter 2 considers the political context by focusing upon neoliberalism and pointing to the ways in which this promotes a very individualistic view of social life. It then goes on to consider one of the key concepts within this book, the competing ideas that children are becomings, or beings. Having done this, the chapter then introduces what we see as three contemporary concepts, shaping childhood in the UK the twenty-first century: well-being; vulnerability, and resilience. We consider that each are important, but it is resilience which may be seen as central to our overall argument, that the taming of childhood has a detrimental impact upon the ways in which children may develop and maintain resilience.

Chapter 3 can be seen as starting with a consideration of what a tame childhood may lead to by discussing the contemporary criticism of young people as snowflakes. Although we are reluctant to accept the idea that snowflake is an accurate description of young people, our experiences in teaching young adults does provide some insight into how it is that such a derogatory term has come to be used with ease. It is commonplace in the universities in which we work for students to request extensions for their assessments several months after the death of a grandparent or explain absence on the basis of a family member being hospitalised. Similarly, many of our students request alternative forms of assessment to avoid undertaking a presentation and many Learning Support Plans, strategies which aim to make education more inclusive, advise staff not to put students 'on the spot' by asking questions.

In making sense of these experiences, it appears to be the case that such individuals have little in the way of resilience. Our general argument is that if children are never challenged, never experience adversity, or never face risks, then it is likely that they will lack resilience. We are arguing that this is often the case and this is because childhood is, or has been, tamed. With that in mind, Chapter 3 moves on from considering the outcomes of taming to establish just what Rittel and Webber meant by wicked and tame, and how we are using tame as an evaluative approach to understand childhood and children's lived experiences.

What should be obvious then is that we are not suggesting that children grow up to be snowflakes because of some inherent weakness or deficiency. Instead, we would point to the way in which contemporary childhood can be seen as impoverished. We are arguing that this is not good for either society or children themselves. What is important to consider though is that this is the outcome of childhood experiences which are shaped by others, usually adults, for children. The first context within which this happens is the family and this is the focus of Chapter 4.

It is worth noting at this point that we have elected to refer to parents/carers as parents throughout and that we tend to view the primary location of children as within a home or family. We recognise that families may adopt a range of forms and practices. We subscribe to the view that families are what families do and that this accommodates different forms. Similarly, we recognise that not all parents care but might also suggest that not all carers do either. As such, we are guilty of adopting a rather tame approach in suggesting that all children will have a home and that someone will have parental responsibility for them. In this book, we refer to these individuals as parents.

There are three key concerns within Chapter 4. The first is the emergence of a somewhat intense and intrusive form of parenting which has come to be referred to as helicopter parenting. Helicopter parenting sees parents playing a major role in children's lives, especially with regard to making decisions. This can be seen as linked closely to the issue of parental surveillance. We consider how the fear of risks intersects with new technologies in ways which sees parents being preoccupied with where their children are. This in turn is reinforced by social concerns regarding what it means to be a good parent. The result of such an approach, however, can be seen in the ways in which children are leading increasingly restricted lives in terms of children's geographies. Many children simply do not play out, especially without adult supervision.

Of the three chapters that can be seen as focused on a particular aspect of childhood, the book begins with the family in Chapter 4. This is because this can be seen as the key influence upon individual children's lives. Chapter 5, however, focuses upon the early years as an important example of how childhood comes to be shaped by the State, and by practitioners as children experience life beyond the family. The idea of children as becomings is clearly shown within policies and practice which are often preoccupied by a view of early years as a transition to education alongside a concern about readiness.

In some ways, the introduction of Every Child Matters (DfES 2004) and the growth of Surestart children's centres may be seen as the colonisation of childhood by the State. As such, it is one way in which childhood becomes more homogenous and becomes further shaped by adults who have a particular view of childhood and becoming in mind. In one sense, it is the Every Child Matters agenda which did much to reinforce the idea of children as vulnerable and which amplifies a sense of risk that is faced by children, accompanied by a growing approach towards surveillance. Following from this, an increasing concern with safeguarding can be seen to have provided justification for the restrictions that have come to be placed upon children under the guise of keeping them safe. Risk has come to represent an unambiguous threat which requires managing. The management of risk though may be seen as having the unintended outcome of producing a tame childhood.

Chapter 6 considers some of the ways in which children's experience of school contributes to the taming of childhood. Although school can be seen as the key site for most children with respect to education, our concerns are not rooted within education itself. Instead, we present school as a site which is increasingly restrictive in terms of children's experiences and in terms of how it restricts their agency. The idea of safeguarding as introduced Chapter 5 is also influential in schools as can be seen in the ways in which children's activities during playtime have been restricted. Children's agency can also be seen to be restricted by considering the ubiquitous nature of school uniform which is presented as a key mechanism by which children are depersonalised within the school system.

Although school uniform is presented as a means by which children's agency is reduced through prohibiting any form of personal expression, developments which can be considered as forms of datafication take this further. The growth of targets within education aligns with views of education as a process within which children come to be cast as having value only in terms of being data points.

In conclusion then, we consider that a number of factors have come to align in ways which have the effect of taming childhood. We do not consider that this is driven by any overarching concern to achieve this. Indeed, many of the policies and practices may be seen as seductive in how they are presented as being beneficial to children. A retrospective evaluation of how numerous changes within children's lives have come to change childhood, however, suggests that children are having fewer opportunities to engage, explore, and challenge their world, fewer opportunities to express their agency. As a consequence, childhood is becoming impoverished. For many children, their childhood is tame.

References

Action for Children. 2018. *Mental Health for Young People* (Online). Watford. Available https://www.actionforchildren.org.uk/what-we-do/our-impact/mental-health-overview/mental-health-for-young-people/. Accessed 18 October 2018.

Aynsley-Green, A. 2018. *The British Betrayal of Childhood*. London: Routledge.

Ben-Arieh, A. 2006. Is the Study of the "State of Our Children" Changing? Re-visiting After 5 Years. *Children and Youth Services Review*, 28, 799–811.

Bradshaw, J. (ed.). 2016. *The Well-Being of Children in the UK*. Bristol: Policy Press.

Bradshaw, J., Hoelscher, P., & Richardson, D. 2007. An Index of Child Well-Being in the European Union. *Social Indicators Research*, 80, 133–177.

Care Quality Commission. 2017. *The State of Health Care and Adult Social Care in England 2016/2017*. London.

The Children's Society. 2018. *The Good Childhood Report 2018*. London.

DfES. 2004. *Every Child Matters: Change for Children/ Department for Education and Skills*. London: Department for Education and Skills.
Foundation, M. H. 2016. *Fundamental Facts About Mental Health 2016*. London: Mental Health Foundation.
Hartog, J., & Oosterbeek, H. 2007. What Should You Know About the Private Returns to Education? In: Hartog, J., & Maassen Van Den Brink, H. (eds.), *Human Capital: Advances in Theory and Evidence*. Cambridge: Cambridge University Press.
James, A. 2009. Childhood Matters: Is Children's Wellbeing a High Enough Priority. *Mental Health Today*, 18.
OECD. 2009. *Doing Better for Children*. Paris: OECD.
Palmer, S. 2009. What Is Toxic Childhood. In: House, R., & Loewenthal, D. (eds.), *Childhood, Well-Being, and a Therapeutic Ethos*. London: Karnac Books.
Palmer, S. 2015. *Toxic Childhood: How the Modern World Is Damaging Our Children and What We Can Do About It*. London: Orion Books.
Rittel, H. W. J., & Webber, M. M. 1973. Dilemmas in a General Theory of Planning. *Policy Sciences*, 4, 155–169.
Sointu, E. 2005. The Rise of an Ideal: Tracing Changing Discourses of Wellbeing. *Sociological Review*, 53, 255–274.
Taylor, D. 2011. Wellbeing and Welfare: A Psychosocial Analysis of Being Well and Doing Well Enough. *Journal of Social Policy*, 40, 777–794.
UNICEF. 1989. *UN Convention of the Rights of the Child* (Online). UNICEF. Available https://www.unicef.org/rightsite/237.htm. Accessed 12 March 2018.
Vincent, C. 2017. "The Children Have Only Got One Education and You Have to Make Sure It's a Good One": Parenting and Parent–School Relations in a Neoliberal Age. *Gender and Education*, 29, 541–557.

2

The Context of Childhood

Abstract Children's lived experiences are shaped by a number of influential ideas about childhood. Since 1979, the political context of the UK has been dominated by **neoliberalism**. This promotes an individualised view of social life, reinforcing in turn an understanding of children as **becomings** rather than beings. Alongside this though, we point to three key concepts that have emerged with respect to how children are seen: **well-being, vulnerability,** and **resilience**. A critical view of each demonstrates how these concepts are forged within social contexts and how they come to be mobilised in ways which often undermine and impoverish childhood, contributing to what has come to be referred to as **snowflakes**.

Keywords Neoliberalism · Becomings · Well-being · Vulnerability · Resilience · Snowflakes

© The Author(s) 2019
R. Creasy and F. Corby, *Taming Childhood?*,
https://doi.org/10.1007/978-3-030-11842-6_2

2.1 Introduction

As was suggested in the introduction, this book puts forward the argument that contemporary childhood can be understood as having been changed in ways which, following Rittel and Weber, we refer to as tame. We are not the first to give some critical commentary upon contemporary childhood. Aynsley-Green, the first Children's Commissioner within the UK, has suggested that Britain has changed in ways that can be understood as a betrayal of childhood (Aynsley-Green 2018). Similarly, Palmer (2007, 2009, 2015) has previously commented upon how social changes have had an impact upon children in a negative way, her most contentious claim being the idea that contemporary childhood is toxic. We are sympathetic to this view, arguing that tameness contributes to a childhood that is impoverished and unfulfilling. The salience of this is that tameness reduces the experiences of the child in ways which undermine the development and maintenance of resilience. This can be seen in growing concerns about an inability to cope with what might be considered as everyday pressures together with an apparent deterioration in the state of mental health amongst children and young people.

In this chapter, we present a number of contexts that either shape childhood, or have come to be associated with childhood and which are particularly relevant to understanding the context within which childhood is subject to taming. We have focused, however, on concepts and issues which are strongly associated with practice, in that we see them as concepts which influence how practice is carried out, whether that be by parents or practitioners. As such, we begin by considering how the political ideology of neoliberalism accentuates the idea of children as individual, especially in relation to the idea of children as being seen on a trajectory towards adulthood. This can be summarised as a view of children as becomings. The opposite to this, the importance of seeing children as beings rather than becomings, is well established in terms of academic debates. We are not convinced that it is as well established in practice and feel that there is some merit in revisiting these ideas here. The chapter draws to a close then by considering some ideas that can be seen as inter-related in the ways that they influence how childhood, and children are understood: well-being, vulnerability, and resilience.

2.2 The Individual Child: Neoliberalism to New Labour

Tobin et al. (2011) demonstrate that, with respect to the ways in which children's development is provided for, this is not generally done in a vacuum, provision tends to be made with an end in mind. So, it can be seen that there tends to be a general understanding at a societal level of what is wanted for children and in respect of what is believed to be appropriate for children within any given society. This is generally based on what any given society would want children to become alongside how children may be understood at any given time in terms of their development. What this does is to demonstrate that there is an understanding that children can be shaped or moulded and that childhood can be or should be provided for in a particular way. This understanding, however, is subject to a range of competing discourses; however, not all voices are heard equally.

Political discourse is particularly pertinent because the political inclinations of any society inevitably shape the policy context of childhood at that time. Within the UK, it is generally accepted that a neoliberal discourse has been embedded within much of UK society over the last 40 years and that this may be seen as emphasising an individualistic way of understanding ourselves. It therefore reinforces the ways in which we see children as individual rather than as being located in, or reflective of, a social position.

Like many countries, the UK has been influenced significantly by neoliberal ideas. This goes back to the election of the first Thatcher government in 1979 and although the Labour governments from 1997 to 2010 may reject the label of neoliberal, it would be wrong to say that they rejected neoliberalism outright. Because of this, we are claiming that neoliberalism has provided a dominant political context since 1979. A full discussion of the political ideology that is neoliberalism is beyond the scope of this short book, but is pertinent to note that neoliberalism is never an ideology that is easy to pin down (Davies 2014; Amable 2011; Turner 2011; Mirowski and Plehwe 2009). It is difficult to arrive at an unambiguous definition of neoliberalism. The range of ideas which constitute neoliberalism inevitably contributes to a degree of confusion. At the same time, something which also contributes to a degree of confusion or uncertainty with respect to neoliberalism is the way in which some commentators reject it as being an invalid concept, or elect to leave it unspoken (Mirowski 2014). Following Foucault though, it can be argued that denying neoliberalism or electing not to voice it only serves to increase its political power. As such, a practical position to take is to see neoliberalism as representing a thought collective (Dean 2014; Mirowski and Plehwe 2009). Seeing neoliberalism as a thought collective is a way of encompassing the ideological aspects of it by considering the ways in which the basic tenets of neoliberalism become embedded within policies and practice. However, it is also the case that, at times, there are inconsistencies and contradictions to neoliberalism that can be recognised (Garrett 2009). These inconsistencies and contradictions do not provide any basis for rejecting the impact of neoliberalism; they merely serve to illustrate how politics as a practice may not accurately reflect the ideological basis that inspires it.

As a thought collective though, we can see how neoliberalism privileges an economic system that is claimed to be a free market and which promotes the idea of parents being engaged in creating the conditions for their children's later success within a competitive environment (Simpson and Envy 2015). Although the neoliberal concern with free markets has been important with respect to social service provision since 1979, it is also important to consider the strong emphasis upon individualism. Neoliberalism rejects a social understanding of society, and, as part of this, explanations for social differences which are rooted in social characteristics such as class, gender or ethnicity are resisted. For neoliberals, all individuals can achieve anything as long as they make the most of their abilities and work hard. This has consequences for the ways in which children are viewed. In this way, neoliberalism gives rise to an understanding of childhood wherein parents are tasked with providing the best opportunities for their children and children are seen as having individual responsibilities to make the right life choices with respect to the opportunities that are open to them. Importantly though, such ideas come to be seen as axiomatic or self-evident and become quite resistant to alternative views.

As neoliberalism privileges the idea of individualism, this tends to negate any concerns for an understanding of the ways in which individual lives are shaped by social structures and/or the individuals place within society. Such a perspective, however, is somewhat unsatisfactory. A naïve reading of individualism appears to overlook the numerous ways in which individuality is repressed within children's lives as their lived world becomes increasingly managed and planned, as it becomes tame.

2.3 Children as Beings or Becomings

In moving from the political context to childhood itself, it seems appropriate to start by claiming that although children are clearly universal, it is obvious that childhood is not. In one sense, children are only universal in existing as a particular, biological, stage in the development of human beings, but what should be evident to all is that as children, they are very often subject to the views and actions of others, especially those who are older. This is because age very often acts to order power, whether that be to bestow it or to negate it (Sundhall 2017). In opening a discussion of children as beings or becomings then, it is worth considering that childhood is always transitory (Gillespie 2013). It may be the case that, as adults we have all experienced childhood, but this is not necessarily the same childhood. The social, political, and cultural context existing at the time that we are children does much to shape how we experience our childhoods and, also, does much to inform the argument being presented here. Much has been written about a sociological perspective of childhood and although appearing radical and fresh at the time, what became known as the new sociology of childhood is now well established (Wyness 2012; Qvortrup et al. 2009; James and Prout 1997).

In one way, this draws attention to the value of using wicked and tame to evaluate childhood. We could say that, in general, childhood is seen from one of two exclusive positions, as being, or as becoming (Wyness 2012; James and Prout 1997). As such, children are caught up in the tension that exists between these, but it is not a simple, or tame, position. The relationship between seeing children as becomings or beings reflects the wicked problem that Rittel and Webber (1973) point to (the ideas of Rittel and Webber will be explored fully in Chapter 3 which follows). Childhood in general can be seen to be influenced on a social level, but children in particular are subject to the behaviours of parents and/or carers which may act against the wishes of children themselves. Parents in particular may be said to want children to have good and innocent childhoods, but they are often caught up within a consideration of what they want their child to become, or what they think their child will need to achieve this. In this way, children never grow and develop solely as a consequence of their own intentions. They are always subject to external forces. This reinforces a view of children as becomings.

The view of children as being puts the focus on the child. As such, it bestows upon children the possibility of agency that is rooted within understanding them as having validity in their own right. By seeing the child as a being, the child is elevated to some extent from a historical position as the property of their parents and comes to occupy an active position with respect to the social construction of their self. Such a position sees children as deserving of rights as per the United nations Convention on the Rights of the Child (UNCRC), (UNICEF 1989) and as being capable of making a valid contribution to society, but that is not to suggest that children automatically benefit from these rights (Baraldi and Cockburn 2018).

It is difficult to reject the view of children as deserving of rights; yet, few parents or practitioners would go so far as to argue that such a position establishes a child's right to self-determination in all matters. Although children's participation in society implies a role within decision-making, we would argue that, within the UK, there is a general reluctance to grant participation in line with the spirit of the UNCRC. For example, although children may want to be able to play, the UK focus on learning means that this becomes a matter of contention (Davey and Lundy 2011). As Lyon (2007) makes clear, in spite of the widespread emphasis given to the UNCRC, children in England are subject to English law and, as such, they do not have claim to all the rights set out within the UNCRC. A view of children as not being capable of making rational decisions contributes to a reluctance to accept children as beings rather than becomings.

In many ways, the emergence of the view that children should be treated as beings in their own right has done much to change the experience of childhood. However, at the same time, the opposite view of childhood, that children are becomings, can be seen as continuing to exercise considerable power and influence, especially when it comes to rights (Cassidy 2012). From the perspective of seeing children as becomings, children are viewed in relation to a future state, namely as adults, though we may also say, a particular type of adult. From this perspective, children are always viewed as lacking or deficient on the grounds that, as children, they have not become fully formed. They come to be seen as occupying a position along a developmental trajectory, which in turn makes possible the consideration of children with respect to potential. In this way, childhood always comes to be seen as secondary to adulthood, though not necessarily as secondary to old age. Although there are strong arguments which seek to reconcile each approach (Uprichard 2008) on the grounds that individually both may be viewed as lacking to some extent, it seems clear that the becomings perspective is one which positions adulthood as the dominant position within ideas about the life course. For example, it is reflected in the way that adults who are seen as not behaving in an acceptable way are often described as childish or immature, etc. Importantly though, we would argue that it is the dominant position as adopted by both parents and practitioners.

This concern with becomings can be seen in a variety of ways and social practices. For example, the commonly heard concern that children should be able to achieve their potential reflects the idea that children are a work in progress. Similarly, the ubiquitous adoption of milestones relating to children's developmental progress can be seen as an approach which easily transforms into a normative device (Fattore et al. 2007). In particular, the way in which an understanding of childhood has been dominated by developmental psychology can be seen to have done much to position children as becomings (Walkerdine 2009).

As such, it is developmental psychology which does the most to provide a structure for identifying success and failure at certain milestone points along the way to becoming.

With this in mind, although we firmly support an understanding of children as beings, we are inclined to suggest that it is not a position that is routinely adopted by either parents or practitioners, as was suggested earlier. We would say that the view of children as becomings remains quite firmly entrenched within the UK.

As an addition to the discussion of children as beings or becomings though, it is also worth considering the ways in which the history of childhood often rests upon such ideas (Hanson 2017). Hanson contributes to academic debates on childhood by drawing attention to the ways in which the history of childhood is often drawn upon to make sense of not only who they are at any given time but also to contextualise future possibilities. For example, Gillespie (2013) demonstrates how poor children in inner city areas of nineteenth-century New York were unwelcome within dwellings as a consequence of overcrowding. The consequence of this was not only that children would spend social time on the streets, they were also inevitably experiencing a social life that was often characterised by encounters with other cultures and other ages alongside the more general interactions of city life. Gillespie points to the ways in which this created social tensions. She goes on to show how a discourse of children as becomings shaped ideas about town planning in ways which intersected with concerns about poor children in particular having too much freedom. To that end, town planners of the time acted in ways which aimed to curtail children's movement for reasons which were deemed to be in the long-term interests of children.

At the same time, legislation aimed at curtailing child labour in both the UK and America could be seen as drawing upon ideas about childhood, and in particular, what was appropriate for children (Heywood 2018). What can seen from these examples then is that in terms of how we understand children and childhood, a concern for children's well-being has a long history.

2.4 Well-Being and Well-Becoming

For a number of years now, it has been difficult to overlook the growing importance of well-being in relation to debates about children and childhood. The influence of well-being has become embedded within a range of policies and services (Children's Society 2018; Bradshaw 2016; Knight et al. 2014; Taylor 2011; Ben-Arieh 2006). At the same time, there are numerous academic papers and books which explore issues relating to well-being, though sometimes the concept is used in a way which suggests that it is axiomatic, that it is unambiguous. This is not the case. For example, the influence of well-being can be seen in the ways in which many large organisations have drawn up and implemented well-being policies, though often this is strongly associated with physical health when the focus on well-being was intended to move away from a medical view of wellness. With this in mind, in a book aimed at supporting well-being in the early years, Roberts (2010) argues that "health and happiness are needed to underpin the kind of childhood that is *every* child's right" (p. 3). In making this claim, Roberts reinforces the idea that well-being is a characteristic of good health, which suggests then that children who experience poor health do not enjoy well-being. She also adopts an unproblematic version of rights. We share her concern with the rights of the child, and that rights should be universal, but we also recognise that rights do not exist in a vacuum. Rights are always the outcome of political struggles. They can be won and lost.

Importantly though, the condition of childhood is often mobilised against children in a way which denies them rights (Cassidy 2012; Wall 2008). Although this statement may appear to be out of step when considering the rise of concerns about children such as the development of a concern for the child's voice, the claim has to be considered within the context that, within England, adults retain the right to hit children in a way that would be illegal should they hit another adult. Similarly, the freedoms of children are often restricted by adults in ways that are not experienced by adults themselves, something that will be considered further in Chapter 4. Furthermore, policies are often put in place that are suggested to be for the good of the child when, in fact, there is no evidence to support this.

We would argue that well-being as individual experience, or subjective well-being, is central to how we are using the term as opposed to the well-being of children as being a universal concept. The Children's Society (2018) defines this as thus: "Subjective well-being can be thought of as a positive state of mind in which a person feels good about life as a whole and its constituent parts, such as their relationships with others, the environments that they inhabit and how they see themselves" (p. 9). Subjective well-being can be seen as adopting a broader and more holistic approach to understanding well-being. This is particularly relevant to the argument that childhood is subject to being tamed, in that taming is often manifest in a reduction of childhood experiences that follow from the increasing restrictions that are brought to bear in terms of what children are permitted to do, very often because of our concerns about what happens to a minority of children.

What soon becomes clear, when considering the idea of well-being is that as a concept, well-being can be seen to be somewhat slippery. It is a contested concept with no firm, or clear definition (Fava et al. 2017; Wellard and Secker 2017; Spratt 2016; Ecclestone and Hayes 2009; Sixsmith et al. 2007). What needs to be established then is that well-being is a complex, multi-dimensional issue (Fava et al. 2017; McNaught 2011). It is perhaps important to note then that well-being is not some fixed state that has to be achieved. The multi-dimensional nature of well-being inevitably means that it is a dynamic concept and that in both objective and subjective terms, it is something that is constantly changing and constantly subject to both internal and external changes. For example, with reference to parent–child interactions, Rönkä et al. (2017) report upon the impact of parental work schedules in three countries. The demands upon parents, and their time, are of importance to the child's life, but it can be seen that parental work schedules may be influenced by both the employer with respect to demands and by the nature of support from a range of sources that is available to parents at any given time, something which may also change as a consequence of political decisions.

In some ways, this slipperiness may increase the attractiveness of a term or label to policy-makers and practitioners. The very lack of definition means that any actions which policy-makers and practitioners deem necessary can be presented as being in the interests of the well-being of the child. At the same time, it can see how well-being is an idea that is hard to resist. It seems nonsensical to claim that anyone wouldn't want to achieve, or support, well-being. As Anderson and Graham (2016) note though, in relation to children, very often, well-being is used in a way that summarises adult aspirations for them rather than children's own understandings of well-being. Similarly, differences can be seen between what adults see as important for children's well-being and what children themselves see as being important (Spratt 2016; Fattore et al. 2007; Sixsmith et al. 2007). There is some relevance here to the concept of helicopter parenting as will be discussed in Chapter 4. The concept of helicopter parenting reflects strong and active involvement in a child's life and, crucially, sees parents making decisions for their children in the belief that this will advantage those children. LeMoyne and Buchanan (2011), however, report that well-being is reduced in children who experience helicopter parenting as a consequence of the strategies being adopted by such parents.

In some ways, a growing focus on well-being may be understood within the context of deteriorating economic conditions experienced by many individuals or families, in that it shifts attention away from a focus upon material wealth or abundance, and on to concerns about individual experience. Although we have no intention of negating the importance and value of well-being per se, it is noticeable that a concern with well-being has become prominent around the time that neoliberal polices are increasingly being seen as insufficient or failing, though Sointu (2005) notes that the everyday use of well-being can be seen as promoting individual responsibilities in a way which reinforces neoliberal views. There is a sense then that a concern for well-being may be mobilised by governments who recognise that neoliberalism has widened inequalities to such an extent that many young people in particular are very likely to experience long-term financial hardship. This is in a context of stagnant, or declining wages in real terms

(ONS 2018), but it may also be as a consequence of insecure and un- or under-employment.

As such, an ostensible concern for well-being, and its associated concern with happiness, may be adopted by a government which is suggesting that it has little aspiration or power to reverse rising inequalities, so instead, turns to an old idea, that it is possible to be poor yet happy. In adopting this position, happiness and economic position or wealth is disconnected, but this is disingenuous, for it is not necessarily the level of economic wealth that is important. Being richer does not necessarily result in greater levels of happiness (Layard 2011) either individually or on a social scale. The issue may be seen as the position regarding economic wealth within a context of inequality (Wilkinson and Pickett 2018). The social consequences of inequality, as opposed to poverty, are well documented by Wilkinson and Pickett (2010). As part of this argument, the impact of inequality on mental health is of concern (James 2009), especially given that the number of children living in poverty has increased as a consequence of policies introduced by the UK Coalition government from 2010 and characterised as "austerity" (Jupp 2017; Lambie-Mumford and Green 2017; Tunstill and Willow 2017; Churchill 2013). Although there are many texts which indicate the nature and consequences for austerity within the UK, these studies in particular demonstrate the impact that such policies are having on families and children. Lambie-Mumford and Green (2017) are particularly pertinent, in that they illustrate the significant growth of children who rely on foodbanks as a direct consequence of government policies.

In this regard then, we might see that although it is inequality that is the key problem, it is also the case that the incomes of the poorest have suffered significant cuts. We are supportive of the idea that inequality should be tackled; the UK is after all one of the richest countries in the world, and if the UK cannot provide a reasonable standard of living for all children, then we wonder who can. However, we would argue that inequality is not the sole determinant that influences children's lives. We have already considered the tensions which exist between seeing children as beings or becomings, but we can also see how the nature of childhood may be subject to more specific ideas such as vulnerability as will be considered next.

2.5 Vulnerability

In terms of how governments have approached well-being with respect to children, it is evident that there is a strong discourse of children being vulnerable or at risk (Wellard and Secker 2017; Turnbull 2016; Turnbull and Spence 2011). This discourse can be seen to have influenced both practice and policy regarding well-being in a way which purports to identify some children as vulnerable. It can also be seen that, in practice, vulnerability is associated with levels of needs with needs being categorised from universal to complex and acute, though a shared understanding of what is meant by vulnerable is often absent (Coram and Coram 2017). Very often though, where vulnerability is referred to, this draws upon either children as naturally vulnerable or children as vulnerable because of experiencing some degree of deprivation.

Poverty and inequality are clearly relevant within any discussion of children's lives. UK policies have long sought to address either poverty, or the consequences of poverty. In recent years though, such policies have often been subject to changes which have involved a move away from the universal provision that was embedded within the Welfare State policies originating in the late 1940s. Instead, there has been a return of sorts to means tested benefits, generally under the guise of being targeted, and with specific political agendas of who is responsible for children living in poverty. The discourse of targeting is quite seductive, in that it draws upon ideas about both desert and need. In this approach, benefits are presented as being provided for those with most need and, in doing so, are presented also as being targeted at those who are deserving of such assistance. Within this approach though, a further concept can be seen to have come to be emphasised, that of targeting the most vulnerable, though importantly this is bound up with the idea that poverty is presented as being synonymous with being vulnerable. From this perspective, poverty acts to constitute those children who live in poverty as being vulnerable. What they are vulnerable to, however, is less clear cut.

An understanding of vulnerability sits very easily in how childhood can be understood and much has been written about the basis of children's vulnerability. As with other concepts which contribute to this argument overall though, vulnerability is very often taken for granted and under-explored. The idea that some within society are vulnerable has come to be seen as in some way natural. Children fit easily within this perspective because of particular characteristics that they may be seen as displaying. Children's size, lack of resources and limited knowledge all are issues that underpin power and which are associated with dependency. They make it very easy for society to conceive of children as innately vulnerable but we have already indicated how age comes to act as an ordering of power (Sundhall 2017). In other words, children are not intrinsically vulnerable just because of size, cognitive ability or resources; instead, it is how these are managed within society.

It may be easy to use this type of explanation when considering the vulnerability of babies or infants, but it is not useful for explaining the position of all children particularly as policy has positioned humans as children up to the age of 18 years. In addition to this though, there is also a need to recognise that becoming labelled as vulnerable is not simply a consequence of other characteristics such as being poor, or being disabled, for example. Being labelled as vulnerable is the consequence of the ways in which social, political, and cultural forces operate to establish a particular version of what it means to be vulnerable (Brown 2017; Brotherton and Cronin 2013). In this way, it can be seen how it is important to understand vulnerability as a characteristic of social relationships and how those relationships are enabled in a way that makes some people, children for example, vulnerable.

The argument that vulnerability exists as a characteristic of social relationships can be seen with respect to an increasing social concern about the need for counselling or other therapeutic interventions. In this respect, the relationship between vulnerability and a general concern with how children and young people cope with the pressures of contemporary life is considered by Furedi (2004). Furedi draws particular attention to the way that an expanding culture of therapeutic interventions does much to nurture the idea that children are vulnerable and that they will respond in a particular way to the experiences that they encounter. Such concerns can be seen to have contributed to the massive growth in therapeutic provision within schools, colleges, and universities (Ecclestone and Hayes 2009).

However, in general, therapeutic interventions require participants to reflect on experiences or to draw upon a range of experiences that enable a participant to put experiences into context in a way that enables them to cope and move on. Children who have been protected or tamed are unlikely to have a range of experiences to draw on. Children need the opportunities to learn how to cope with difficulties and failure on a small scale to enable them to deal with bigger difficulties or failures as they get older. If it is assumed that children are vulnerable per se, then there is a danger that they are prevented from having the opportunities for them to gain experience through trying difficult things.

It can also be recognised that other contemporary discourses contribute to the idea that children are vulnerable. McNamee (2016) demonstrates how socially accepted ideas about what is best for children may contribute to outcomes which are not good for some children. In this way, McNamee demonstrates that it is not age that creates vulnerability, it is ideas about childhood and how society responds to those ideas. As such, we can reiterate that vulnerability exists within a social context rather than being an individual trait. In reinforcing an idea of vulnerability though, we would point to how this operates in parallel with the idea of resilience, especially with the idea that lacking resilience increases vulnerability. As was established above, our argument is that the taming of childhood reduces the opportunities that children have to encounter setbacks or adversity and that this undermines their ability to develop and maintain resilience.

2.6 Resilience

Having previously established the importance of a growing concern with well-being, we argue that a key aspect of achieving well-being is the ability to be resilient. As such, the idea of resilience is very pertinent to the argument being presented within this book. In a simple sense, resilience is generally understood as an individual's ability to cope with, or bounce back from, adversity (Garrett 2018; Frydenberg 2008). In this way, resilience can be seen to be important for anyone's ability to live within the social world. It is inconceivable to think that any of us will not experience some adversity or setback at some stage within our lives. Importantly though, experiencing adversity is essential to building resilience.

Contemporary ways of understanding resilience can often be seen to be rooted in views about character and can be summarised as trait approaches. This compares to developments which posit resilience as an outcome or process (Fletcher and Sarkar 2013). As with other concepts relating to social life though, resilience can also be said to be a slippery concept (Martínez-Martí and Ruch 2017; Ecclestone and Lewis 2014; Taket et al. 2014). As was said earlier, concepts can be said to be slippery when they are hard to define. The difficulties in establishing an objective definition, or understanding of resilience, are identified by Russell (2015) who notes that "Definitions offered by research psychologists often reflect their preoccupations" (p. 162).

There are a number of relevant factors in considering resilience. Olsson et al. (2003), in a consideration of adolescence, do much to demonstrate the different approaches that can be taken towards understanding what resilience is. They also point to the role of well-being in terms of understanding resilience and in the importance of considering social factors. As such, they draw attention to the tensions between seeing resilience as a characteristic or possession compared to seeing it as a process. By viewing resilience as a process, it comes to be understood in a broader sense, in that it ceases to be a characteristic that any individual has, or does not have, and comes to be seen in a more dynamic sense (Hamilton 2011). As such, this draws attention to those factors which may contribute to an individual being able to build resilience (Taket et al. 2014). This is generally presented as being the outcome of the interplay of three factors usually identified as being the individual, the family, and the community, though there is a danger that this ignores some more general influences such as policy or media. Even so, adopting this approach provides a much better understanding why some children will cope, and others will apparently not cope, with the same type of adversity.

In returning to the first section of this chapter though, on how the political context of childhood shapes how we understand resilience, Garrett (2018) demonstrates how resilience has come to be mobilised by advocates of neoliberalism in a manner which reflects victim blaming. Garrett points to the ways in which the context of neoliberalism is one of increasing individualism and how explanations for disadvantage come to be explained in terms of personal failing rather than as a consequence of social structures. In this way, the disadvantaged individual becomes cast as an individual who lacks resilience, someone who lacks the ability to navigate the modern world and who fails to achieve because of this. Developing and maintaining resilience through childhood then is clearly important. However, as we have already established that children may be cast as vulnerable because of their position as children, we may start to see how the role of parents comes to the fore.

The role of parents, especially in terms of the early years, clearly impacts upon how children develop and it is not surprising to see parenting styles that may be judged to be intrusive being associated with contributing to low levels of resilience in children (Taylor et al. 2013). At the same time, a consideration of the interplay of different factors recognises that each child has some degree of agency which will influence a degree of variation of experience as well as the possibility of change (Hamilton 2011). In both cases, the political focus becomes what is happening within the family, rather than the conditions within which the family lives.

So, although we have some reservations regarding the way in which resilience is defined and used, we support the concept in a broad sense. Individuals do need to be able to cope with aspects and incidents in their lives which produce some level of adversity. It has been noted that adversity can often be implied to be something of major significance (Fletcher and Sarkar 2013) when, in fact, there are many low-level adversities that we all encounter on a fairly regular basis. Contemporary life can be stressful, but the evidence provided relating to increased mental illness amongst children and young people may be seen as an indicator of increased stressors combined with fewer opportunities to build resilience through encountering or dealing with factors which may contribute to stress. With this in mind, the following chapter will consider the emergence of the use of the term "snowflake" to refer to young people who appear to lack any ability to deal with criticism or stress as reflecting a consequence of our argument, i.e. that childhood is being tamed and that this is not in the best interests of either children or society.

References

Amable, B. 2011. Morals and Politics in the Ideology of Neo-Liberalism. *Socio-Economic Review*, 9, 3–30.
Anderson, D. L., & Graham, A. P. 2016. Improving Student Wellbeing: Having a Say at School. *School Effectiveness & School Improvement*, 27, 348–366.
Aynsley-Green, A. 2018. *The British Betrayal of Childhood*. London: Routledge.
Baraldi, C., & Cockburn, T. 2018. Introduction: Lived Citizenship, Rights and Participation in Contemporary Europe. In: Baraldi, C., & Cockburn, T. (eds.), *Theorising Childhood: Citizenship, Rights and Participation*. Cham: Springer.
Ben-Arieh, A. 2006. Is the Study of the "State of Our Children" Changing? Re-visiting After 5 Years. *Children and Youth Services Review*, 28, 799–811.
Bradshaw, J. (ed.). 2016. *The Well-Being of Children in the UK*. Bristol: Policy Press.
Brotherton, G., & Cronin, T. M. 2013. *Working with Vulnerable Children, Young People and Families*. London: Routledge.
Brown, K. 2017. *Vulnerability and Young People: Care and Social Control in Policy and Practice*. Bristol: Policy Press.
Cassidy, C. 2012. Children's Status, Children's Rights and 'Dealing with' Children. *The International Journal of Children's Rights*, 20, 57–71.
The Children's Society. 2018. *The Good Childhood Report 2018*. London.
Churchill, H. 2013. Retrenchment and Restructuring: Family Support and Children's Services Reform Under the Coalition. *Journal of Children's Services*, 8, 209–222. September.
Coram, & Coram, I. 2017. *Constructing a Definition of Vulnerability—Attempts to Define and Measure*. London.
Davey, C., & Lundy, L. 2011. Towards Greater Recognition of the Right to Play: An Analysis of Article 31 of the UNCRC. *Children and Society*, 25, 3–14.

Davies, W. 2014. *The Limits of Neoliberalism: Authority, Sovereignty and the Logic of Competition.* London: Sage.
Dean, M. 2014. Rethinking Neoliberalism. *Journal of Sociology*, 50, 13.
Ecclestone, K., & Hayes, D. 2009. *The Dangerous Rise of Therapeutic Education.* London: Routledge.
Ecclestone, K., & Lewis, L. 2014. Interventions for Resilience in Educational Settings: Challenging Policy Discourses of Risk and Vulnerability. *Journal of Education Policy*, 29, 195–216.
Fattore, T., Mason, J., & Watson, E. 2007. Children's Conceptualisation(s) of Their Well-Being. *Social Indicators Research*, 80, 5–29.
Fava, N. M., Li, T., Burke, S. L., & Wagner, E. F. 2017. Resilience in the Context of Fragility: Development of a Multidimensional Measure of Child Wellbeing Within the Fragile Families Dataset. *Children and Youth Services Review*, 81, 358–367.
Fletcher, D., & Sarkar, M. 2013. Psychological Resilience: A Review and Critique of Definitions, Concepts, and Theory. *European Psychologist*, 18, 12.
Frydenberg, E. 2008. *Adolescent Coping: Advances in Theory, Research, and Practice.* London: Routledge.
Furedi, F. 2004. *Therapy Culture: Cultivating Vulnerability in an Uncertain Age.* London and New York: Routledge.
Garrett, P. M. 2009. *'Transforming' Children's Services? Social Work, Neoliberalism and the 'Modern' World.* Maidenhead, UK: Open University Press.
Garrett, P. B. 2018. *Welfare Words: Critical Social Work & Social Policy.* London: Sage.
Gillespie, J. 2013. Being and Becoming: Writing Children into Planning Theory. *Planning Theory*, 12, 64–80.
Hamilton, W. 2011. Young People and Mental Health: Resilience and Models of Practice. In: O'Dell, L., & Leverett, S. (eds.), *Working with Children and Young People: Co-constructing Practice.* Basingstoke: Palgrave Macmillan.
Hanson, K. 2017. Embracing the Past: 'Been', 'Being' and 'Becoming' Children. *Childhood*, 24, 281–285.
Heywood, C. 2018. *A History of Childhood.* Cambridge: Polity Press.
James, A. 2009. Childhood Matters: Is Children's Wellbeing a High Enough Priority. *Mental Health Today*, 18.
James, A., & Prout, A. 1997. *Constructing and Reconstructing Childhood: Contemporary Issues in the Sociological Study of Childhood.* London: Falmer Press.

Jupp, E. 2017. Families, Policy and Place in Times of Austerity. *Area*, 49, 266–272.

Knight, A., La Placa, V., & Mcnaught, A. (eds.). 2014. *Wellbeing: Policy and Practice*. Banbury: Lantern.

Lambie-Mumford, H., & Green, M. A. 2017. Austerity, Welfare Reform and the Rising Use of Food Banks by Children in England and Wales. *Area*, 49, 273–279.

Layard, R. 2011. *Happiness: Lessons from a New Science*. London: Penguin.

Lemoyne, T., & Buchanan, T. 2011. Does 'Hovering' Matter? Helicopter Parenting and Its Effect on Well-Being. *Sociological Spectrum*, 31, 399–418.

Lyon, C. M. 2007. Interrogating the Concentration on the UNCRC Instead of the ECHR in the Development of Children's Rights in England? *Children & Society*, 21, 147–153.

Martínez-Martí, M. L., & Ruch, W. 2017. Character Strengths Predict Resilience Over and Above Positive Affect, Self-Efficacy, Optimism, Social Support, Self-Esteem, and Life Satisfaction. *The Journal of Positive Psychology*, 12, 110–119.

Mcnamee, S. 2016. *The Social Study of Childhood*. London: Palgrave.

Mcnaught, A. 2011. Defining Wellbeing. In: Knight, A., & Mcnaught, A. (eds.), *Understanding Wellbeing: An Introduction for Students and Practitioners of Health and Social Care*. New York: Lantern Publishing.

Mirowski, P. 2014. *The Political Movement That Dared Not Speak Its Own Name: The Neoliberal Thought Collective Under Erasure*. Available https://www.ineteconomics.org/uploads/papers/WP23-Mirowski.pdf. Accessed 11 October 2016.

Mirowski, P., & Plehwe, D. (eds.). 2009. *The Road from Mont Pèlerin: The Making of the Neoliberal Thought Collective*. Cambridge, MA: Harvard University Press.

Olsson, C. A., Bond, L., Burns, J. M., Vella-Brodrick, D. A., & Sawyer, S. M. 2003. Adolescent Resilience: A Concept Analysis. *Journal of Adolescence*, 26, 1–11.

ONS. 2018. *Statistical Bulletin: UK Labour Market: February 2018 Estimates of Employment, Unemployment, Economic Inactivity and Other Employment-Related Statistics for the UK*. London: Office for National Statistics.

Palmer, S. 2007. *Detoxing Childhood: What Parents Need to Know to Raise Happy, Successful Children*. London: Orion.

Palmer, S. 2009. What Is Toxic Childhood. In: House, R., & Loewenthal, D. (eds.), *Childhood, Well-Being, and a Therapeutic Ethos*. London: Karnac Books.

Palmer, S. 2015. *Toxic Childhood: How the Modern World Is Damaging Our Children and What We Can Do About It.* London: Orion Books.
Qvortrup, J., Honig, M.-S., & Corsaro, W. A. 2009. *The Palgrave Handbook of Childhood Studies.* Basingstoke, NY: Palgrave Macmillan.
Rittel, H. W. J., & Webber, M. M. 1973. Dilemmas in a General Theory of Planning. *Policy Sciences*, 4, 155–169.
Roberts, R. 2010. *Wellbeing from Birth.* London: Sage.
Rönkä, A., Malinen, K., Metsäpelto, R.-L., Laakso, M.-L., Sevón, E., & Verhoef-Van Dorp, M. 2017. Parental Working Time Patterns and Children's Socioemotional Wellbeing: Comparing Working Parents in Finland, the United Kingdom, and the Netherlands. *Children and Youth Services Review*, 76, 133–141.
Russell, J. S. 2015. Resilience. *Journal of the Philosophy of Sport*, 42, 159–183.
Simpson, D., & Envy, R. 2015. Subsidizing Early Childhood Education and Care for Parents on Low Income: Moving Beyond the Individualized Economic Rationale of Neoliberalism. *Contemporary Issues in Early Childhood*, 16, 166–178.
Sixsmith, J., Gabhainn, S. N., Fleming, C., & O'Higgins, S. 2007. Children's, Parents' and Teachers' Perceptions of Child Wellbeing. *Health Education*, 107, 511–523.
Sointu, E. 2005. The Rise of an Ideal: Tracing Changing Discourses of Wellbeing. *Sociological Review*, 53, 255–274.
Spratt, J. 2016. Childhood Wellbeing: What Role for Education? *British Educational Research Journal*, 42, 223–239.
Sundhall, J. 2017. A Political Space for Children? The Age Order and Children's Right to Participation. *Social Inclusion*, 5, 164–171.
Taket, A. R., Nolan, A., & Stagnitti, K. 2014. Family Strategies to Support and Develop Resilience in Early Childhood. *Early Years: An International Journal of Research and Development*, 34, 289–300.
Taylor, D. 2011. Wellbeing and Welfare: A Psychosocial Analysis of Being Well and Doing Well Enough. *Journal of Social Policy*, 40, 777–794.
Taylor, Z. E., Eisenberg, N., Spinrad, T. L., & Widaman, K. F. 2013. Longitudinal Relations of Intrusive Parenting and Effortful Control to Ego-Resiliency During Early Childhood. *Child Development*, 84, 1145–1151.
Tobin, J., Hsueh, Y., & Karasawa, M. 2011. *Preschool in Three Cultures Revisited: China, Japan, and the United States.* Chicago, IL: University of Chicago Press.

Tunstill, J., & Willow, C. 2017. Professional Social Work and the Defence of Children's and Their Families' Rights in a Period of Austerity: A Case Study. *Social Work & Social Sciences Review*, 19, 40–65.

Turnbull, G. 2016. The Price of Youth: Commodification of Young People Through Malleable Risk Practices. *Journal of Youth Studies*, 19, 1007–1021.

Turnbull, G., & Spence, J. 2011. What's at Risk? The Proliferation of Risk Across Child and Youth Policy in England. *Journal of Youth Studies*, 14, 939–959.

Turner, R. S. 2011. *Neo-Liberal Ideology: History, Concepts and Policies*. Edinburgh: Edinburgh University Press.

UNICEF. 1989. *UN Convention of the Rights of the Child* (Online). UNICEF. Available https://www.unicef.org/rightsite/237.htm. Accessed 12 March 2018.

Uprichard, E. 2008. Children as 'Being and Becomings': Children, Childhood and Temporality. *Children & Society*, 22, 303–313.

Walkerdine, V. 2009. Developmental Psychology and the Study of Childhood. In: Kehily, M. J. (ed.), *An Introduction to Childhood*. 2nd ed. Maidenhead: Open University Press.

Wall, J. 2008. Human Rights in Light of Childhood. *International Journal of Children's Rights*, 16, 523–543.

Wellard, I., & Secker, M. 2017. 'Visions' for Children's Health and Wellbeing: Exploring the Complex and Arbitrary Processes of Putting Theory into Practice. *Sport, Education and Society*, 22, 586–601.

Wilkinson, R., & Pickett, K. 2018. *The Inner Level: How More Equal Societies Reduce Stress, Restore Sanity and Improve Everyone's Wellbeing*. London: Allen Lane.

Wilkinson, R. G., & Pickett, K. 2010. *The Spirit Level: Why Equality Is Better for Everyone*. London: Penguin.

Wyness, M. G. 2012. *Childhood and Society*. Basingstoke: Palgrave Macmillan.

3

Introducing Tameness

Abstract The claimed failings of young people, such as a heightened sense of sensitivity and an apparent lack of **resilience**, have led to them being referred to as **snowflakes**. This can be seen as the consequence of a tame childhood, wherein **risk** has been removed from children's lives and where children are increasingly restricted in what they can do. Contemporary discourses relating to children, **childcare**, and **parenting** act as rules which regulate our understanding of each and that what follows from these understandings are practices that shape the lives of children. This is used to introduce the idea of **tameness** as found within the work of Rittel and Webber.

Keywords Resilience · Snowflakes · Risk · Childcare · Parenting · Tameness

3.1 Introduction

Chapter 2 presented a range of issues that we see as relevant to the context of childhood in the UK in the twenty-first century. We are not saying that these are the only relevant issues, but we do see them as being particularly influential with respect to how childhood is now understood. Each has relevance to the general argument that is being put forward, namely that childhood is being subject to a process of taming and that the taming of childhood undermines the development of resilience. This then leads to consequences which are not in the interests of children. This chapter will develop this idea through introducing the concept of snowflakes as an example of how children may be affected by the taming of childhood. It will then go on to consider the concept of taming as per the work of Rittel and Webber.

We are arguing that the consequences of the taming of childhood are reflected to some extent in the term "snowflake generation", adults coming of age in recent years who are said to both lack resilience and be hyper-sensitive. The matter of resilience, as was introduced in Chapter 2 is of importance to this argument. The fact that some children may be experiencing problems in developing resilience may be indicated to some extent by the growing demands for child and adolescent mental health services.

In some ways, there is a growing tension which emerges from a view of growth being associated with children having emotional problems and where an increased awareness or concern with emotional well-being leads to a growth in the availability of services. As children come to be seen as experiencing emotional problems, it is of little surprise that there is an increase in the numbers of children deemed to be experiencing them, as part of this, though emotional problems come to be seen as something which requires expert help to address in a way that is analogous to physical health. The solutions to emotional problems are then seen to come from the intervention of experts rather than being something that is available in the family, from friendships or within the local community.

We are not proposing that mental health is wholly social in nature, but we are arguing that not having the opportunities to develop resilience may weaken any child's ability to deal with the adversities that they may experience. Alongside this, international comparisons recognise that childhood in the UK is often qualitatively poorer than in other Western countries. It is not that taming is being argued as having defined consequences but, rather, that taming may be used to assess how children experience their lives. Importantly though, concerns with resilience and well-being have increased as has been illustrated previously. Though these may be seen as demonstrating a recognition of the pressures of contemporary life, they do not in themselves provide for a retrospective evaluation of social life. The concept of taming does.

The main aim of this chapter then is to demonstrate the value of employing the concepts of wicked and tame to childhood. It does this through substituting wicked and tame with wickedity and tameness. The idea of social issues being seen as wicked or tame originally emerged in the work of Rittel and Webber (1973). Their original focus on wicked problems is evident in many papers relating to contemporary debates; however, it can be seen that each type of problem is relational. We can only really understand them in terms of how they differ from each other. That said, we should not see wicked and tame as constituting a dichotomy; instead, we will argue that it is more useful to consider these as forming a continuum. The main aim of this chapter is to establish the value of tameness as a concept with regard to understanding childhood.

What was evident from Chapter 2 is that whilst we are not arguing that childhood should be seen as a process, it is the case that ideas about development and the raising of children tend to posit childhood in this way. This can be seen in relation to achieving particular milestones or outcomes. As such, children are often understood as human becomings rather than human beings as has been discussed previously. Academic debates demonstrate that there are advantages to a more holistic approach, viewing children as both becomings *and* beings, but policy and practice can be seen as drawing from the idea of becomings to a much more significant degree. At the same time, practice may be seen as existing within a number of competing discourses. These discourses may posit children as both becoming and being, whilst prioritising, we will argue, becoming. Whilst considering and recognising the academic debates regarding the value of adopting a more sophisticated model of understanding childhood, the book draws from practice experience in considering contemporary experiences of childhood. The aim here is to provide insight into how policy and practice, which may be taken for granted within contemporary discourses, may lead to unintended outcomes. In this sense, we will argue that generation snowflake is just such an unintended outcome.

3.2 Snowflakes

The term snowflake when used in the particular, or snowflake generation in a general sense, is used in a derogatory manner. It has emerged relatively recently within the UK and is more typically used to refer to young adults rather than children, especially, but not exclusively, to students. Snowflake students are characterised as overly sensitive to criticism or challenge and being generally lacking in resilience. This may be seen in claims that they resist views which do not correspond to their own and that they are requiring of warnings before being faced with material which they may find distressing (*Times* 2017). The relevance of considering snowflakes here is that this is generally applied to young adults who have experienced a process of becoming throughout their childhood. If so, the mental state of this generation does not appear to be anything that could be seen as desirable.

Some caution is perhaps necessary, however, with regard to the term snowflake. It is a term which can be seen to be used by right-wing commentators whilst resonating with the left, such as Fox (2016), at the same time. That said, in the UK, most commentaries on the snowflake generation are to be found in right-leaning, in political terms, or populist newspapers such as the *Daily Mail* and *The Times* and draw on examples which may not be typical. As such, the term snowflake, or snowflake generation, may be seen as a discursive device used to negate children and young people's concerns and experiences. In this way, the term snowflake comes to act as a pejorative term representing the weaknesses, or failings, of young people to have developed in ways that are desirable. It draws attention away from the context of childhood as socially structured and locates it in the individual as some kind of personal weakness.

We would argue, however, that whenever such a discursive device arises, there is often something worth considering further. The question that has to be asked is why is it that young people are, or are said to be, appearing to struggle with certain issues in such large numbers that a terminology arises to account for it? Although cautious about adopting this terminology, the book as a whole will explore further the ways in which the taming of childhood can be seen to contribute to a lack of resilience.

Underpinning this are concerns about resilience. In one sense, resilience can be seen to be analogous with medical inoculations. The principle behind inoculation is, of course, that a mild infection provides the basis for future resistance. In this way, children would need to encounter some adversity in their lives if they are to develop resilience. With reference to the understanding of resilience as the consequences of the interplay between the individual, the family, and the community, then we can start to see how a community which has come to see adversity as risk and which becomes preoccupied with risk aversion will impact upon family and parenting practices.

As a consequence, it is reasonable to consider that parents become drawn into being risk averse and that because of this, children become far less exposed to adversities than was once the case. This is something that will be evident within later chapters. As will be argued throughout the book, this can be understood as the taming of childhood and it operates in ways to change the lived experiences of children in a manner which means that children are increasingly denied opportunities to develop resilience. One reason for this is that, very often, encountering risk is promoted as something that children cannot cope with or understand. Because of this, the encountering of risk comes to be seen as something that should not form part of the good childhood that parents and practitioners feel that they should be providing for children. Children come to be seen as needing protecting from risk; thus, their life becomes increasingly tame. This 'tameness' should be of concern because we would argue that a tame childhood is not in the child's best interests and, ultimately, we are arguing that this is not in society's interests either.

However, at the same time that it can be seen that as parents are become more risk averse and increasingly restricting the activities of their children, as a consequence, this is being accompanied by a growing level of hyperbole relating to the praise that parents are encouraged to heap on their children (Suissa 2013). Parents seem to be constantly praising their children when they do rather mundane things. This is possibly as a result of parenting strategies that rely on positive praise rather than negative challenge. The consequences of parental over-valuation (Brummelman et al. 2015) are that it seems no longer sufficient to refer to a child's abilities or achievements as good, they are always amazing or incredible. Storr (2017) discusses this as the consequences of a social movement concerned to increase self-esteem. Whether or not praise works to improve outcomes is not clear. Some studies indicate that this is the case (Gunderson et al. 2013, 2018). Lee et al. (2017), however, note that the relationship between praise and achievement is not straightforward. It may be the case that parents need to distinguish between extraordinary achievements and everyday functioning. Furthermore, these achievements are very often based on a limited range of activities; activities that are supervised and part of a prescribed process of becoming such as educational outcomes and sporting achievements alongside more mundane everyday activities.

What results though is children being increasingly praised for doing or achieving what is somewhat mundane whilst being denied the challenges that would contribute to the development of resilience. Children then may develop self-esteem, but they do it within a context where they are rarely challenged and within an environment which does not present any risk. This does not bode well for when challenge does arise.

In considering self-esteem as part of a general discussion about resilience and vulnerability, it is also pertinent to point to the ways in which this intersects with the political context and, in particular neoliberal ideology. We have said previously that neoliberalism promotes an individualistic outlook; intrinsic to this are ideas about the naturalness of social competition. UK society has become increasingly more competitive and this competitiveness influences everyday relationships including parenting, seen in increased examples of competition amongst parents.

It can also be argued that the actions of parents who bestow exaggerated praise upon their children are linked to the idea raised earlier regarding children as becomings. If parents are acknowledging the competitive nature of society that has been intensified as a consequence of neoliberal policies, their exaggerated praises may be seen as attempts to create a level of confidence in their children that will provide some bulwark against the harsh reality of a free market society. In this way, such an approach to parenting appears reasonable, but if children's self-esteem is not in line with their actual abilities, this may prove problematic. It may be that praise actually becomes mundane or meaningless when it bears little relationship to what children have really achieved. This seems to us to be the perfect conditions for the development of what has been termed snowflakes; young people and adults who over-estimate challenge and who may avoid situations that to them are uncomfortable. The paradox is that we have a situation where it appears that children receive more praise but are able to actually do far less as a consequence of the restrictions placed upon them as part of the taming of childhood. To explain this further, it is pertinent to establish what we mean by taming.

3.3 Conceptualising Issues as Wicked or Tame

The defining of problems as either wicked or tame begins with the work of Rittel and Webber (1973) in response to issues related to urban planning. It has since been applied to diverse concerns, some of which may be seen as tangentially related to childhood such as Health (Burman 2018; Gronholm et al. 2018; Blackman et al. 2006), Education (Creasy 2018; Jordan et al. 2014; Wright 2011; Bore and Wright 2009; Knight and Page 2007), and Social Policy (Hayden and Jenkins 2014).

Undertaking a basic library search provides numerous journal articles drawing upon the concept of wicked problems, suggesting that the growing use of this approach offers some indication of its usefulness in terms of evaluating contemporary issues. This is particularly the case with issues which can be seen as complex because of their social roots. The basic premise of the concept is that some problems have clear or obvious solutions whilst others are much more complicated. For Rittel and Webber, tame problems are indicative of the type of issues where outcomes are obviously right or wrong. Wicked problems, however, reflect complexity and relativity.

It would be erroneous, however, to infer that such a position means that tame problems are simple. They may be quite complex yet subject to unambiguous rules with respect to how they are addressed and in terms of what will be recognised as a successful solution (Bottery 2016).

For example, an engineering project may pose challenges, but the knowledge that we have regarding the physical properties of materials means that it can be understood as tame in terms of the approach taken by Rittel and Webber. So, if we were tasked with constructing a table that would be suitable for our classroom, we could ascertain the weights and stresses that are likely to applied to it and, knowing the properties of certain materials, construct a workable table. In itself, this is not only tame, it is also simple. If the task was to process nuclear materials, the physical properties still lead to the problem being tame, in that they are known and therefore the problem is still subject to procedures with an obvious end result, even though there is a degree of complexity that was absent within the first example.

From the perspective of wicked and tame, the examples may differ in complexity, but they remain tame, something that can be seen as applying to all problems that are accommodated within a scientific perspective. In many ways, science, as an approach, seeks tameness if the term is seen as reflecting certainty. When it comes to social issues, however, there is a degree of complexity and uncertainty that accompanies such concerns (Stevens and Hassett 2007) and which means that tameness becomes elusive. Following Rittel and Webber, any social policy issue is inevitably a wicked problem as will be explained further below. As such, issues to do with how society engages in the practice of raising and educating children are wicked because of the range of factors involved and the intrinsic lack of certainty. Practitioners will encounter this in respect of the diverse ways that children may react to the situations that they find themselves in. Although it is often claimed that children are all unique, we can point to many aspects of policy and practice which overlook this fact, sometimes for good reasons, and which seek to treat children as simple rather than complex. This can be evidenced by our inability as a society to protect children from harm despite considerable policy and practice put in place to address this.

Bottery (2016) adds to our understanding of wicked problems in pointing out that in relation to any issue which involves social behaviour, there is often a degree of complexity which means that understanding problems in causal ways, such as is found within scientific problems, is often insufficient. This may be seen within contemporary approaches to social policy. In spite of increasing levels of bureaucracy and the establishment of standardised practices, human activities are generally characterised by consequences which are frequently both unexpected and unintended. Significant time and effort may be put into reducing unexpected and unintended outcomes, but humans are not automatons and their behaviour is often at odds with what may have been anticipated or planned. At the same time, there is often little agreement regarding the policy matters that are under scrutiny.

The problem, from the perspective of wicked and tame, is that the aims of social policy are now often associated with values or intentions which may not be shared, problems which may not be self-evident and matters such as equity which may not be consensual. However, what can be seen is that those professionals charged with addressing such policy issues have often taken direction from a scientific paradigm, a paradigm which works well when materials are inanimate, but which is patently inappropriate in situations where plurality and reflexivity are intrinsic features of the parties involved. At this point, it is worth considering just what we mean by the term paradigms, as it can be argued that what Rittel and Webber are engaged in is making a case against adopting a paradigmatic approach which is inappropriate.

3.4 From Paradigms to Evidence-Based Practice

In one sense, this section appears to be quite a departure from the idea that childhood is, in some way, being tamed, but it does have relevance to an understanding of the basis of Rittel and Webber's concept of wicked problems. Within social science, the concept of paradigms is well established. It originates within the study of science in the seminal work of Kuhn (1996). In a basic sense, Kuhn presents a paradigm as an organising principle. This is commonly seen in respect of understanding research in respect of how any particular research method can be established as valid (Plowright 2011). In research, the epistemological position adopted by a researcher can mean that the validity ascribed to one method then has the effect of invalidating alternative methods. With respect to the idea of wicked problems, it can be seen how an approach that has been shaped by a scientific perspective may be problematic when dealing with social issues.

So, Kuhn's concept of paradigms may be seen as relevant when considering social practices such as parenting and with regard to child development. For example, consider how individuals, working within disciplines, come to develop communities of practice which share ontological and epistemological approaches with reference to the practice of research (Brew 2001). Kuhn argues that one of the defining characteristics of a paradigm is its ability to shift or supersede a previous paradigm: this can be seen in how notions like resilience or 'snowflake' appear, take hold, and then dissipate over time. But in relation to this, not only have ideas about knowledge, and the methods used to generate knowledge, changed over time, it can be seen that there are ongoing struggles which privilege some methods whilst reducing the impact of others. This may be recognised in the way that evidence-based practice has emerged as a principal way of understanding ways of working. More will be said about this later.

Kuhn's focus was on the development of science and consequently, scientific ways of understanding the world. It would be difficult to argue against the benefits of science, but it is the privileging of a scientific approach that Rittel and Webber see as problematic. This is particularly relevant where a scientific approach is applied to situations that do not follow the logic of science such as matters of social policy. At the heart of the argument that Rittel and Webber are putting forward is a concern with the ontological and epistemological arguments that are evident within debates about research.

Such an idea is central to what Gage (2007), writing about approaches to understanding education, has called "the paradigm wars". This draws attention to the tensions which exist between researchers adopting different approaches towards the development of knowledge and understanding. This is epitomised in comparing those researchers engaged in quantitative research to those engaged in qualitative research. As such, each may be seen as working within a separate paradigm. What the work of Rittel and Webber contributes is to draw attention to how scientific approaches, which work well with what they refer to as tame problems, are inappropriate when applied to situations which are social in nature. This is because social issues, as has been argued, involve a level of complexity that undermines a tame solution.

This is not to suggest that Rittel and Webber reject scientific approaches. That is not the case. Their concern is with the degree to which an approach is appropriate and how the adoption of an approach that is not appropriate is very likely to fail. For example, the successes of projects within town planning, such as the provision of utilities, or the establishment of paved roads, are essentially tame. Problems such as these, however, can be seen to be qualitatively different from problems which are linked to social behaviours. What Rittel and Webber address is the way in which the success of approaches to town planning issues, which may be seen as focused on utilities, has led to town planners adopting such approaches even when the nature of the problem has changed. For Rittel and Webber, the fact that some approaches end up being adopted more readily than others leads to a situation whereby some projects will inevitably fail because of the mistaken belief that social problems can be tackled in the same way that scientific problems can be tackled.

In considering why such approaches have been so readily adopted, it is worth considering that scientific approaches towards problems are often very seductive. Historically, they have often produced results which have had significant, and positive, impacts upon our lives.

Rittel and Webber acknowledge this, pointing to how clean water and power may be provided to urban areas, how many diseases have been effectively eradicated as a consequence, and how thousands of individuals are moved around towns and cities smoothly. It is because of these types of successes that some will seek to replicate the successes of a scientific approach. Following from this, it is possible to see how political discourse may favour particular approaches even where the problem itself is one that has changed and where the subject matter is not inanimate materials but individuals.

This can be illustrated by considering the scientifically based research movement in the USA (Denzin and Lincoln 2008) and the rise of evidence-based practice within the UK (Hammersley 2007; Strelitz 2013). In both cases, an increased focus upon the role of evidence can be seen to be seeking to replicate disciplines such as medicine. However, although such an approach may be well suited, and wholly appropriate, to medicine, its value within the wider children's workforce, where practitioners work with far less certainties regarding how children respond to intervention, is consequently far less obvious.

It can also be seen how work with children becomes contentious where different agencies are involved. The development under New Labour of multi-agency working has much to commend it, but it also brings together practitioners with different concerns and different ideas about evidence. Consider how Health Visitors, with their roots being in a medical background, have significant involvement and responsibilities in the early years. This makes them a strong force in support of evidence-based practice with significant influence on early years practice as a whole. What Health Visitors may accept as evidence, however, is not necessarily what other groups would accept.

Arguments in support of evidence-based practice in social occupations such as work with children are neatly summarised by Ravitch (1998) where she draws upon her own experience of being admitted to hospital to contrast the ways in which the medical profession makes use of research compared to what happens within education. Within this comparison, medicine is presented as resting upon certainties; certainties which are known because of research. This sees Ravitch presenting medicine favourably and as being something which education could learn from. In doing this though, Ravitch overlooks the very real differences in respect of the subject that is being researched, in that although human biology does not always respond to medicine in uniform ways, there is clearly a much greater degree of certainty than with respect to how different children respond to teaching.

The position being adopted by Ravitch appears to take a rather narrow view of education which ignores the complexity that is evident when considering the social and cultural contexts of children's lives and how this has some bearing upon education. As such, we can see how medicine is tamer than education. Practitioners who work with children are often faced with a greater degree of complexity because children's lives are complex. However, as has been said, our concern within this book is to assess the extent to which practices which shape the context of children's lives can be seen to contribute to the taming of childhood. We are not seeking to deny the existence of certainties per se with respect to children, but we do seek to emphasise that reducing the scope of their experiences and treating them as automatons rather than individuals will rarely be helpful.

3.5 The 10 Properties of Wicked Problems

The argument at the heart of this book is the idea that policies and practices which relate to children are increasingly leading to experiences of childhood that are tame. This section will say more about the concept of wicked and tame problems as first outlined by Rittel and Webber (1973). It will then consider how this may be developed further so that it may be understood as a continuum. A consideration of Rittel and Webber's original work illustrates that we can see that they considered that a wicked problem lacks the clarity or certainty that is evident within tame problems. For this reason, wicked problems are endemic to social and public policy. Because of this, it is not possible to assert that there will be a clear, or unambiguous, end-state. At the same time, we cannot claim that any solution that is arrived at is intrinsically right or wrong. For Rittel and Webber, it is not that *the* solution has been found; instead, it is simply that *a* solution has been found. This may well be as a consequence of time or financial constraints, but alongside this, there is a further, very important, caveat; that is that with respect to wicked problems, there is no intrinsic quality to the problem by which it is characterised.

What Rittel and Webber are pointing to here is that rather than the problem possessing some intrinsic quality which will act as a reference point, the problem is, instead, defined by the perspectives of the individuals who are engaged with it. Because of this, not only can the problem itself be contested, so can the ideas about how to address it, and even what will be accepted as a satisfactory outcome. Wicked problems then are bound up with political issues in ways which mean that evidence is rarely unambiguous, something which is pertinent when faced with calls for evidence-based practice (Strelitz 2013). Furthermore, what policy-makers and practitioners do tends to have real consequences for individuals and it is for this reason that Rittel and Webber argue that when it comes to wicked problems, there can be no right to implementing the wrong solution. Getting it wrong is rarely acceptable.

In summarising their understanding of wicked problems then they identify what they consider to be the ten defining characteristics of them:

1. Wicked problems have no definitive formulation;
2. Wicked problems have no stopping rules;
3. Solutions to wicked problems cannot be true or false, only good or bad;
4. There is no immediate and no ultimate test of a solution to a wicked problem;
5. Every solution to a wicked problem is a 'one shot' operation, because there is no opportunity to learn by trial and error, every attempt counts significantly;
6. Wicked problems do not have an enumerable (or an exhaustively describable) set of potential solutions, nor is there a well-described set of permissible operations that may be incorporated into the plan;
7. Every wicked problem is essentially unique;

8. Every wicked problem can be considered to be a symptom of another problem;
9. The existence of a discrepancy representing a wicked problem can be explained in numerous ways. The choice of explanation determines the nature of the problem's resolution;
10. The planner has no right to be wrong.

3.6 Wickedity as a Continuum

The concept of wicked problems has grown in influence, though it is often the case that it is used in a manner which assumes a clear dichotomy. This can be seen in the way that Wexler (2009) has suggested. Wexler presents the distinction between tame and wicked problems as a table, shown below:

Tame problems	Wicked problems
Relatively easy to define and can be treated as separate from other problems and the environment	Relatively difficult to define and cannot be easily separated from other problems and the environment
Information needed to solve or make sense of the problem is readily available, well structured, and easy to put into use	Information needed to solve or make sense of the problem is ill-structured, changing, and difficult to put into use
There is a consensus not only among problem solvers over what is the best method but also those with the problem accept and agree with the legitimate problem solvers	There is neither a consensus among problem solvers over what is the best method nor a clear agreement over who is and is not a legitimate problem solver
This class of problems has precedents from which one can learn or take advice from others in order to become a "bona fide" problem solver	These problems are unique and changeable; therefore, attempts to solve them make learning difficult and progress towards a solution erratic
Stakeholders to the problem defer to the expertise of the problem solver and seek little or no say in the process beyond that requested	Stakeholders to the problem join the problem solvers in possessing conflicting views of the problem, its solution, and the degree of involvement of the problem stakeholders

Wexler may be seen as accepting of the dichotomy that is intrinsic to the initial formulation of wicked and tame problems. In doing this though, the complexity of many issues is overlooked. As Bottery (2016) states, "it would in some ways be attractive if it were always possible to distinguish between simple and tame problems, and so to always know with certainty with which kind one was dealing. But this is unlikely to be the case, as many problems are likely to be mixtures of tame and wicked issues, and separating them out will be extremely problematic, and on some occasions even impossible" (p. 45). As a consequence, a much more useful model is provided if we see wicked and tame as two ends of a continuum whereby wickedity falls at one end and tameness at the other. To see wicked and tame as part of a continuum helps to transform the concept from something which is essentially descriptive into something which is evaluative. This can be illustrated if we take the first of Wexler's issues and apply it to a consideration of something that is giving us cause for concern with respect to the behaviour of a child that we work with or care for:

Relatively easy to define and can be treated as separate from other problems and the environment	Relatively difficult to define and cannot be easily separated from other problems and the environment

It may well be the case that the behaviours that have drawn attention to the fact that the child is experiencing some problems or difficulties can be understood as similar to issues that we have experienced before; however, the social context of the child's life may also mean that what has worked previously, or with others, to overcome a similar problem is not as successful in this case. So, where Rittel and Webber provide us with the original concept of problems as being wicked or tame, we adopt the position that the real value of their work lies in it being reconceptualised as wickedity or tameness as alluded to above. This allows us to liberate the approach from something that is focused on particular problems and repositions it as a characteristic of any system or provision. Tameness is quite easy to understand. It is a system whereby there is uniformity, there are certainties. Wickedity encompasses complexity and uncertainty. It represents a system whereby not only are uniformity and certainty not present, as with children, but it may also be that they are not wanted.

For example, an approach to providing for children which removes uncertainty because uncertainty may pose risks has the consequence of removing opportunities for the child to develop resilience and to find strategies with which to accommodate the unexpected. We suggest that this is not in the long-term interests of the child. For example, Chapter 2 introduced the idea of potential, suggesting that this has become a powerful concept in relation to understanding children and their achievements. However, it has to be recognised that for a child to reach their potential, there has to be some degree of challenge and challenge is generally associated with risk. Reducing risk then is likely to reduce challenge and have a negative impact upon what a child may achieve.

Furthermore, the argument being presented here is that if both wickedity and tameness can be understood as characteristics of systems, this can be used to evaluate the outcomes or consequences of providing for children as a whole. In such an evaluation though, it is important to establish that from this perspective a greater degree of wickedity is seen as desirable and tameness is seen as undesirable. With this in mind, we adopt the position that a tame childhood is not desirable. Why that is the case has already been suggested: tame experiences are impoverished experiences and will do little to assist a child in developing and maintaining resilience. In concluding this section, the analytical value of considering wickedity and tameness means that it may be applied to different aspects of how we provide for children. That may be as practitioners, policy-makers, or parents.

3.7 Conclusion: The Possibility of Childhood

In conclusion, this chapter has illustrated the way in which the original conceptualisation of wicked problems (Rittel and Webber 1973) can be developed as an evaluative tool through which to approach many issues. The concerns of this book are that we use the concept of wicked and tame to assess the extent to which childhood is becoming tame as a consequence of policies and practices which either seeks to remove uncertainty from children's lives or which act to restrict the scope of children's experiences. This is not to fall into the trap of presenting either children or their experiences as homogeneous. We are well aware that both children and their experiences can be understood as individual in very many ways. At the same time though, the social and political contexts of children's lives are such that there are powerful discourses which act upon children, practitioners, and parents. Because of this, we can point to the ways in which the individuality of each party, children, practitioners, and parents, should be understood as existing within certain parameters and that these parameters can and do change.

In this sense, Foucault's concept of conditions of possibility is pertinent (1989). In considering the idea of conditions of possibility, we can see how contemporary discourses relating to children, childcare, and parenting act as rules which regulate our understanding of each and that what follows from these understandings are practices that shape the lives of children. Because of this, we can appreciate that childhood does not remain fixed, that although as adults we all have experienced childhood, that does not provide sufficient grounds for us to claim that we know what it is like to experience childhood now.

Therefore, the childhood that we experienced and the childhood that children now, or at any time, experience is always produced within certain conditions of possibility. Of course, one thing which contributes to these conditions of possibility is our (adult) reflections on our own childhoods. Importantly though, that does not necessarily mean that adults may restrain from acting upon children in ways which, we argue, restrict their experiences in comparison to our own. We might. In restricting what children do now though adults, especially as parents, may be seen as responding to changes with respect to ideas about the condition of both childhood and of what it means to parent. This idea may be extended further with respect to practice. The practice of child care and education is always shaped by the conditions under which it is produced. These may be discursive or based in policy frameworks. They may be subject to political decisions at a range of levels from concerns about accountability or the impact of managerialism within the workplace to supra-national ideas such as the UNCRC. The key point being that there is nothing natural or inevitable about how society provides for children, nor how childhood is experienced, it is always shaped by political, social, and cultural factors.

We would claim that in spite of differences at the level of each child's life, discourse shapes the conditions of possibility in such a way that all children are acted upon to a greater or lesser extent and that in turn, this does create general trends which means that general conclusions can be drawn. As far as this book is concerned, the general conclusion is that developments in policy and practice, and we include parenting within practice, have increased the tameness of childhood. An increasing concern with well-being and with respect to children developing and maintaining resilience illustrates why it is that we should be concerned about tameness.

References

Blackman, T., Elliott, E., Greene, A., Harrington, B., Hunter, D. J., Marks, L., Mckee, L., & Willimas, G. 2006. Performance Assessment and Wicked Problems: The Case of Health Inequalities. *Public Policy and Administration*, 21, 66–80.

Bore, A., & Wright, N. 2009. The Wicked and Complex in Education: Developing a Transdisciplinary Perspective for Policy Formulation, Implementation and Professional Practice. *Journal of Education for Teaching*, 35, 241–256.

Bottery, M. 2016. *Educational Leadership for a More Sustainable World*. London: Bloomsbury.

Brew, A. 2001. *The Nature of Research: Inquiry in Academic Contexts*. London: Routledge.

Brummelman, E., Thomaes, S., Nelemans, S. A., de Castro, B. O., & Bushman, B. J. 2015. My Child Is God's Gift to Humanity: Development and Validation of the Parental Overvaluation Scale (POS). *Journal of Personality & Social Psychology*, 108, 665.

Burman, C. J. 2018. The Taming Wicked Problems Framework: A Plausible Biosocial Contribution to 'Ending AIDS by 2030'. *The Journal for Transdisciplinary Research in Southern Africa*, 14, e1–e12.

Creasy, R. 2018. *The Taming of Education*. Basingstoke: Palgrave Macmillan.

Denzin, N. K., & Lincoln, Y. S. 2008. Introduction: The Discipline and Practice of Qualitative Research. In: Denzin, N. K., & Lincoln, Y. S. (eds.), *Strategies of Qualitative Enquiry*. 3rd ed. London: Sage.

Foucault, M. 1989. *The Archaeology of Knowledge*. London: Routledge.

Fox, C. 2016. *I Find That Offensive*. London: Biteback.

Gage, N. 2007. The Paradigm Wars and Their Aftermath: A 'Historical' Sketch of Research on Teaching Since 1989. In: Hammersley, M. (ed.), *Educational Research and Evidence-Based Practice*. London: Sage.

Gronholm, P., Henderson, C., & Gronholm, P. C. 2018. Mental Health Related Stigma as a 'Wicked Problem': The Need to Address Stigma and Consider the Consequences. *International Journal of Environmental Research and Public Health*, 15, 1158.

Gunderson, E. A., Gripshover, S. J., Romero, C., Dweck, C. S., Goldin-Meadow, S., & Levine, S. C. 2013. Parent Praise to 1- to 3-Year-Olds Predicts Children's Motivational Frameworks 5 Years Later. *Child Development*, 84, 1526–1541.

Gunderson, E. A., Sorhagen, N. S., Gripshover, S. J., Dweck, C. S., Goldin-Meadow, S., & Levine, S. C. 2018. Parent Praise to Toddlers Predicts Fourth Grade Academic Achievement Via Children's Incremental Mindsets. *Developmental Psychology*, 54, 397.

Hammersley, M. (ed.). 2007. *Educational Research and Evidence-Based Practice*. London: Sage and The Open University.

Hayden, C., & Jenkins, C. 2014. 'Troubled Families' Programme in England: 'Wicked Problems' and Policy-Based Evidence. *Policy Studies*, 35, 631–649.

Jordan, M. E., Kleinsasser, R. C., & Roe, M. F. 2014. Wicked Problems: Inescapable Wickedity. *Journal of Education for Teaching*, 40, 415–430.

Knight, P., & Page, A. C. 2007. *The Assessment of 'Wicked' Competences*. Milton Keynes: Open University Practice-Based Professional Learning Centre.

Kuhn, T. 1996. *The Structure of Scientific Revolutions*. Chicago: University of Chicago Press.

Lee, H. I., Kim, Y.-H., Kesebir, P., & Han, D. E. 2017. Understanding When Parental Praise Leads to Optimal Child Outcomes: Role of Perceived Praise Accuracy. *Social Psychological and Personality Science*, 8, 679–688.

Plowright, D. 2011. *Using Mixed Methods: Frameworks for an Integrated Methodology*. London: Sage.

Ravitch, D. 1998. What If Research Really Mattered? *Education Week*, 18, 33.

Rittel, H. W. J., & Webber, M. M. 1973. Dilemmas in a General Theory of Planning. *Policy Sciences*, 4, 155–169.

Stevens, I., & Hassett, P. 2007. Applying Complexity Theory to Risk in Child Protection Practice. *Childhood: A Global Journal of Child Research*, 14, 128–144.

Storr, W. 2017. *Selfie: How We Became So Self-Obsessed and What It's Doing to Us.* London: Picador.

Strelitz, J. 2013. "It Sounds Good But...": Children's Centre Managers' Views of Evidence-Based Practice. *Journal of Children's Services*, 8, 21–30. March 15.

Suissa, J. 2013. Tiger Mothers and Praise Junkies: Children, Praise and the Reactive Attitudes. *Journal of Philosophy of Education*, 47, 1–19.

Times. 2017. Snowflake Generation Seek Solace in Safe Spaces. *The Times.*

Wexler, M. 2009. Exploring the Moral Dimension of Wicked Problems. *International Journal of Sociology and Social Policy*, 29, 531–542.

Wright, N. 2011. Between 'Bastard' and 'Wicked' Leadership? School Leadership and the Emerging Policies of the UK Coalition Government. *Journal of Educational Administration and History*, 43, 17.

4

Home and Family

Abstract Changes within **parenting** have seen an intensification of parental involvement in children's lives. A context of children as becomings against a backdrop of risk has led to parents being involved in decision-making to a much greater extent and to an increased level of **supervision**. The rise in **helicopter parenting** acts to impoverish childhood and restrict children's agency. Children's access to spaces beyond the home contributes to a sense in which childcare is concerned with containment. Being a **good parent** then becomes dominated by **surveillance** with a focus on knowing where children are and what they are doing at all times. This leads to a tame childhood where opportunities to develop are restricted

Keywords Parenting · Supervision · Helicopter parenting · Good parent · Surveillance

4.1 Introduction

The argument that runs through this book is that for many children within the UK, their lived experiences are contributing to what we are calling a tame childhood. We see this as being problematic as we are arguing that this impoverishes children's ability to develop resilience and that this also has an impact upon their well-being. In making this argument, we suggest that taming operates at different levels, from general social trends such as concerns about risk, to the actual practices of such as parents and schools. In this chapter, we focus on the home and consider some of the ways in which family life and parenting contribute towards the taming of childhood. One important aspect of this is with respect to how children's spaces are increasingly restricted. Children within contemporary UK society in general have less scope than in previous generations with respect to where, how, and with whom they may spend their time, as well as where they are permitted to go and where they are welcome.

In considering the ways in which children have come to live increasingly restricted lives, this can be considered as being a consequence, initially, of the ability of parents to exert power over their children. The idea that parents have power over their children is something that might be seen as so obvious it needs no stating. It can see, however, that this power may be employed in two basic ways: the power to compel children to act in a certain way and the power to prevent them from acting in a certain way. What should also be recognised though is that the exercising of such power, in either case, does not happen in a vacuum. As Smith (2014) demonstrates, when power is exercised over others, this is always within a broad framework which conceptualises not only how others are viewed and understand but also how they may react to power being exercised upon them. In this way, if, as we suggest, parents primarily see children as becomings, they are likely to exert power over them within a context of what they see as appropriate for their children and how their children will develop. In itself though, this is not sufficient to explain how parents act towards their children. Smith (2014) also argues that what parents do is a consequence of the ways in which a number of discourses intersect. This then translates into how children experience their lived world.

In discussing ways in which the home and family experience influences the future lives of children, great care must be taken to avoid the easy path that is a deterministic explanation. By this, we mean the sort of explanation which suggests that children's behaviour, character, and achievements, or the lack of them, can be explained by invoking their parental influences. That said, in family life, as well as in practice and policy, we see the idea that children are the direct product of their parent being promoted. Former prime ministers have justified the need for early intervention on the basis of family conditions. Tony Blair's "warnings" regarding the unborn children of single-parents provide a real reminder of how determinism can be evidenced within approaches to social policies (Garrett 2018). For David Cameron (2011), it is "troubled families" who produce the children which go on to commit vandalism and crime. Very often, however, there is an explicit link that is made in which it is families who experience poverty, or families headed by lone parents, who are seen as being the most problematic (Garrett 2009; Romagnoli and Wall 2012; Sayer 2008). What has become evident over recent decades then is that parenting has changed and that it has become a legitimate focus for social policy (Veltkamp and Brown 2017; Vincent 2017; Corby 2015; Romagnoli and Wall 2012).

The real problem with the sort of deterministic arguments provided by Blair and Cameron is that they present families and parenting as causal explanations. This is not the case. Although parents do exert significant influence over their children, as children get older, they become subject to other influences such as peers, schools, and the media. So, although we reject this simplistic, deterministic approach, we do not deny that parenting has influence. But furthermore, parenting is also influenced by a number of factors and parenting styles and attitudes that can be seen to change over time. What we will present within this chapter is a consideration of a number of ways in which changes with respect to parenting have had an impact upon the lived world of the child. As such, our argument is not that children grow up to be reflections of their parents but rather that parents have significant influence upon the range of experiences which contribute towards a child's development.

As part of this, we point to ways of parenting which limit the child's experiences and which contribute to the argument that childhood is being tamed.

4.2 Parents and the Place of Children

One view of parenting that has grown in importance in recent decades is the idea that parenting requires intervention (Lewis 2011). This can be seen as influencing social policies as is illustrated in the comments attributed to Blair and Cameron above. This is not to suggest that social policies aimed at parents and families are new. Lewis notes that advice and guidance aimed at parents are not a recent development, but she illustrates a change in their focus by showing how, in England, the early twenty-first century saw the development of parenting policies being established in an interventionist manner. As part of this development, it can be seen how parents have often come to be considered as lacking in some way; they have started to be seen through the lens of a deficit model to the point that societal problems such as youth crime and educational failure are seen to be failures, if only in part, of parents.

In considering a deficit model of parenting, within a society with a heightened awareness of risk, problems relating to childhood often come to be explained in terms of the threats to children from their environment which parents need to be aware of and protect their children from. What follows from this is that events which impact negatively upon children are often explained as being the consequences, of deficient parenting. This can be seen as particularly evident within tragedies such as the abduction and/or abuse of children by strangers. What is relevant in such cases is that such incidents come to be viewed as a consequence of a weakness or failure in parenting, but, importantly, where parenting is seen predominantly with respect to supervision. As a society, there is a general recognition that some individuals pose a threat to children and that as a consequence, we should expect parents to take action to protect their children from this threat. This often means that the claims regarding a perceived deficiency in parenting tend to take precedence over the actions of the perpetrator. The consequence is that in a society which promotes parenting as supervision, there is a greater possibility that children spend very little time unsupervised. If we consider that unsupervised time creates greater opportunities for free play, then it can be understood how it is that children are losing opportunities to develop as individuals through opportunities to free play either alone or with peers. Because of this loss of social opportunities, childhood is likely to become stifled within supervisory parenting, something which will be considered further, later.

In the example provided above, the issue of threat is external, but it can also be considered how children themselves may be seen as a threat and how this also comes to be viewed as the consequence of parental failings with consequences for taming (Garrett 2009; Sayer 2008). Children who are considered to be misbehaving in a public sphere may be considered to be enabled to do so as a result of failing parents. Even where children are seen to be threatening a social view of children being understood as the sole responsibility of parents can be identified with policies and practices developing in response to this. An example of this is how the practice of establishing Dispersal Orders (Crawford 2009; Crawford and Lister 2008), and the subsequent Public Spaces Protection Orders (Cockcroft et al. 2016; Johnstone 2016) provides scope for the police to disperse groups of young people and gives them the power to return young people to their homes regardless of whether the child has been deemed to have done anything criminally or lawfully wrong (Children's Commissioner 2013). Public Spaces Protection Orders do much to contribute to the reducing of children's geographical spaces and, in doing so, this reduces opportunities for social interaction with peers, something that is a vital part of development. It is perhaps ironic then that adults complain of children being glued to computers and mobile phones whilst ignoring the restrictions that have increasingly been placed on children's physical interactions and opportunities to explore the world beyond their own home.

It is also pertinent to note, however, that very often children seek to undertake social interactions in places which are intended for use by wider society such as shopping or leisure centres. The attraction to children of ostensibly public spaces such as shopping malls and leisure centres may seem obvious, given that they are designed to be attractive, but these are often privately owned spaces (Zhang 2017). Children may not be welcome in such places if they are not behaving in a manner which suits the operators of such spaces. However, there is also a growing move towards seemingly public spaces such as city squares and town centres being privately owned or managed (De Magalhaes and Trigo 2017). In such places, neither children nor anyone else has a 'right' to be there. Both examples contribute to the ways in which a social understanding of the proper place for children is manifest. Importantly though, as children are restricted more and more in terms of being supervised, this impacts further on how they are perceived when they are in these public and private spaces without adult supervision.

In sum, contemporary legislation and practice legitimise the location of children within the home rather than on the street and construct a very different childhood from that experienced by previous generations. Children spending leisure time outside of the home, especially time that is unsupervised on the street, have come to be cast in a negative light. This intensifies an understanding of parenting as supervisory. Very often, the driver is for parents to be able to reassure themselves that they are a good parent, a concern that is relatively new but which can be seen to stem from the way in which parents are judged within society via media, as well as by professionals and government. Importantly though, the 'good parent' has a particular meaning associated with keeping children safe.

As well as becoming more anxious about risk, parents seem to have become more anxious about their own abilities as parents, something which also has consequences for childhood. A historical view of children at home over the previous century and a half reveals a changed position regarding children and it seems counterintuitive to argue that children are being tamed within the home when compared to the harsh punishments meted out to children in previous generations alongside old-fashioned concerns that children should be seen but not heard. An ongoing concern over the continued right to smack children, however, reveals deep-seated views regarding the legitimacy of power over children (Kish and Newcombe 2015; Freeman and Saunders 2014; Brownlie and Anderson 2006).

What can be seen is that over recent decades, a number of competing discourses intersect and influence a situation whereby, against an increasing concern with rights, many children have come to live very restricted lives. For example, the discourse of risk, as mentioned earlier, has become prominent in a way that sees parents and carers reducing opportunities for children to play unsupervised and acting to restrict the spatial boundaries of children's worlds. This can be understood alongside an intensification of schooling which comes to dominate ideas about what children should be doing and sees the school colonising the home through strategies such as homework and learning agreements both of which may be seen as attempts to safeguard against the risk of future failure in a worldview of children as becomings not beings.

As well as changes with respect to risk and education, there have been other changes within approaches towards parenting which have a normative effect and which place increased pressure on parents to be a "good" parent. This generates peer pressure amongst parents and can lead to a competitive element to parenting. It can be seen as being manifest in households where for many children their lives are managed and scheduled, from play-dates for the very young to a range of after-school activities for older children, something which Vincent and Maxwell (2016) refer to as the 'responsibilisation' of parenting. Although one factor which drives this can be seen as the influence of seeing children as becomings within a competitive environment, it can also be argued that is a further aspect to this type of parenting. Irrespective of how some activities may be packaged and presented with respect to the benefits for children, it can also be seen that the provision of a range of activities also affords value to parents with respect to how they may display their parenting. This extends to the idea of family activities, in that a good parent will play with and entertain their children. This is something which is viewed positively but which means that such activities are always supervised.

As such, the home comes to play a significant part within taming but one which is focused on containment. Social pressures to supervise children's engagement with the wider community, alongside public spaces, such as parks, coming to be viewed as threatening mean that children spend more time within the home. At the same time contemporary children may not experience solitude within the home in the way that older adults may once have done. Although solitude has some positive aspects (Stern 2014), children are not necessarily alone at home, and alongside this, solitude is rarely promoted in a positive manner. Very often, parents see solitude as problematic, particularly when solitude involves technology rather than traditional pastimes, such as reading. As such children may be spending more time in the home so that parents are able to claim knowledge of their whereabouts but still be connected to others in a remote manner. What we will see in the following section, however, is that the reach of parents may often extend beyond the home.

4.3 Helicopter Parents

For most children in Western countries, their parents will have a significant influence upon how they experience their lives. Because of this, any consideration of the ways in which children are coming to live tame lives is compelled to consider, to some extent, the role that parents have played. In considering how parenting has changed over time, we can consider how parents have become much more involved with children within contemporary society than was the case in the past. For Kish and Newcombe (2015), the late 1950s saw a change, away from parents acting harshly towards their children, especially in matters of discipline, and towards a more child-centred approach. Such a change was not uniform across society though but we can see a change in general regarding the place of children within families and the actions of parents. In contemporary society, this is promoted and supported by policy approaches such as the ways in which schools seek to work with parents and the ways in which Children's Centres actively sought out partnership working with parents. Much of this is underpinned by governmental approaches, especially those of the Labour governments between 1997 and 2010. In practice, there has been a growing discourse within the UK that revolves around parents being involved in the lives of their children that can be traced back to the 1960s (Bridges 2010) that could now justifiably be referred to as over-involved.

Our experiences in teaching students on undergraduate courses in child and youth studies over a number of years reveal the dominance of a discourse about parenting within which parents are consistently said to want and love their children and to always want the best for their children. This seems to be unquestioned as a general notion about family. There are two weaknesses to this oft-repeated claim. The first is that if all parents want the best for their children, and its associated claim that parents will naturally do anything for their children, then there would no longer be any need for child protection or safeguarding policies. The annual litany of children who are neglected, abused, and harmed by their parents provides an easy way of critiquing this claim. The reason for it being something that is often overlooked or ignored is probably because it does not sit easily with the dominant discourse of family as being a place of care and concern.

The second weakness, however, may be seen as resting upon the ways in which many of our students, parents, and non-parents can point to behaviours which seem to support the claim but which, in practice, have a negative consequence. Furthermore, even when parents recognise this, they may not feel able to change their behaviour for fear of being seen as bad parents or going against what they feel that society expects of them. It is this argument which surfaces quite frequently within this book. We do not doubt that many parents, certainly not all parents, want what is best for their children. We also agree that parental involvement is beneficial for children in a range of ways. What is important is how that involvement is experienced. It may be that sometimes there is just too much parental involvement (Schiffrin et al. 2015). The problem of too much parental involvement is that this often leads parents to behave in ways which have unintended, negative, consequences (Vota 2017; Van Ingen et al. 2015). This can be seen in the phenomenon that is often referred to as helicopter parents or helicopter parenting (Bristow 2014). In this scenario, the relationship that is fostered as a consequence of helicopter parenting reduces the child's ability to develop as an individual (Perry et al. 2018). This then increasingly restricts the capacity of children to function autonomously. The behaviours which characterise helicopter parenting are summarised by Padilla-Walker and Nelson (2012) as "parenting that is high on warmth/support, high on control, and low on granting autonomy" (p. 1178). They present this as a new type of parenting. In a consideration of helicopter parenting typically the focus on warmth/support is rarely commented upon with the emphasis in most commentaries being on hovering, a readiness to become involved, and a tendency towards proxy decision-making.

The helicopter parent can be seen to have emerged as a response to a range of anxieties that are generated within modern society (Bristow 2014; Stearns 2003). The consequence of this though is a type of parenting that can be seen as stifling (Perry et al. 2018; Marano 2004). Both Perry et al. and Marano point to a range of consequences for children which emerge as a consequence of replacing child-directed activity with adult-directed activities. With respect to the helicopter parent–child relationship, there is often a concern with both educational and behavioural outcomes. However, in focusing upon the relationship between helicopter parenting and educational outcomes, LeMoyne and Buchanan (2011) report that strategies which are adopted by parents may well see their children achieving higher grades whilst at college or university, but such strategies may not be to their long-term benefit if it means that this prevents children from developing the types of skills which they will need in later life. At the same time, a focus on educational outcomes is likely to restrict opportunities to develop a range of other skills and attributes that would be of benefit in the long term.

This means that many children are guided by their parents to a far greater extent than was the case for previous generations and so when it comes to exercising their own agency, their ability to act effectively or confidently is reduced or removed. Parents see their child as an object to be managed and not as a person who needs guidance to enable them to act autonomously. Within this model of parenting, the concern to achieve the best outcomes for the child sees childhood becoming distorted into a parental project. As a project though, the parent is minded to exert control over the child so as to ensure the outcome that they desire. This returns us to the idea that was raised in Chapter 2 relating to children being seen as becomings rather than beings. In Chapter 2, we argued that this idea, although resisted within academic debates, has strong significance within family life. In this way, we can see how parents may become inclined to contribute to the taming of childhood as they endeavour to pursue their own agendas and to protect their reputation as 'good parents' by focusing on what their child will become.

Some papers on helicopter parenting draw attention to the way in which it comes to be highlighted when children leave the home to go to university (LeMoyne and Buchanan 2011; Marano 2004). This may be understandable, as this is often the first time that parents have been separated from their children for an extended period. It is also often the first time that the child will have the freedom to act autonomously and be in a position to make their own decisions, something which may also cause concern for helicopter parents. However, the effect of helicopter parenting can be seen to extend beyond university. Peluchette et al. (2013) detail the wider impact of helicopter parenting by considering the effect that it can have in the workplace as parents struggle to let their children become autonomous workers. This may range from low-level helicopter parenting involved with information gathering and providing advice about jobs to more intrusive approaches such as attending job interviews and seeking to influence negotiations about jobs and benefits. What this comes to mean is that in some ways then, the conventional ideas about age and the transition to adulthood no longer apply in some families as parents struggle to let go of their children.

What this means at a societal level is that, in the UK, childhood is becoming ever more extended. This is not only as a consequence of the de facto extension of the school leaving age, nor of the decline in available jobs for young people, it is also because parents are reluctant to acknowledge that their children are adults and are encouraged by new social norms to cling to their child's childhood. As always though, this suggests a somewhat simplistic, or one-way, explanation of the development of helicopter parenting. Fingerman et al. (2012) however, add a further dimension to the rise of helicopter parenting, suggesting that it is often encouraged by children themselves, especially in relation to the provision of financial support. In this sense, it is children themselves who exert influence upon parents based upon the adult child's view of what it means for their parents to be good! Conversely, in return for children behaving as their parents expect, children may seek rewards well into what previous generations would have deemed adulthood and independence. For children then, helicopter parenting may not necessarily be experienced negatively and, in considering their own experiences with those of their peers, it may not seem unusual. What does appear obvious though is that children, even adult children, have less freedom or autonomy than was the case for their parents. Times have changed.

4.4 Parental Surveillance

So, in echoing the work of Kuhn, as discussed in Chapter 3, it can be argued that there has been a paradigm shift with respect to parenting. Changed economic conditions can be seen to have increased instability and reduced security for many as is illustrated by the rise of the gig economy. Alongside this neoliberalism promotes an ideology of individual responsibility that is divorced from economic structures in a cultural sense. Within this context, parenting comes to be seen as a project and becomes intensified.

In considering the rise, no pun intended, of the helicopter parent, it can be seen how the conditions of the early twenty-first century align with contemporary technologies to make helicopter parenting possible, maybe even inevitable. This is not to say that this alignment produces helicopter parenting per se, but it does mean that contemporary discourses relating to both risk and parenting become reasonable, or normalised practices, especially in the context of contemporary communication technologies. This reiterates the Foucauldian concept of conditions of possibility that was introduced in Chapter 3. As such, helicopter parenting is not a style of parenting that was necessarily inevitable, but a number of factors have contributed to it.

One factor though is more relevant to reinforcing it than driving it: developments in communications technologies. For example, if we consider the widespread adoption of mobile phone technology, this can be seen as being encouraged by parents and welcomed by children albeit for potentially different reasons. For children and young people, the phone provides communicative access to their friends, though for children experiencing bullying that may not always be welcome. For parents though, the mobile phone may have greater significance in terms of being able to contact children and, as such, remain connected in case they are needed (Bond 2010, 2013). The first smartphone was released in the mid-1990s, a little over 30 years ago. It would have been hard to imagine then how the development and use of apps would progress. By 2019, however, the helicopter parent has easy access to surveillance and tracking apps such as Life360 (Hasinoff 2017), which use GPS to inform parents of their child's location.

In terms of parenting, what was argued earlier is that in contemporary society, the definition of being a good parent is closely aligned to the parent knowing where their child is. Hasinoff (2017) evaluates the development of apps which perform the function of providing information identifying where children are. In a similar article about the ways in which children are subject to surveillance because of the opportunities offered by new technologies, Simpson (2014) is explicit in stating that there is "a tension between the need to protect children from harm and the rights of the children to develop their autonomy" (p. 273). In this definition though, it is important to state that harm is defined as something that others may cause to children. A cultural concern about the threats that children face then can be seen to have resulted in parental behaviours which restrict children's geographies (Pain 2006). Such restrictions though inevitably impact upon children's access to the spaces that they require to grow.

So, although a key focus within this chapter concerns the home, in considering childhood, we can also see how the extent to which children move beyond the home is important. This may be in terms of going to friends and playing out, though it may also be in terms of going to school or in carrying out errands. Parents inevitably play a role in determining when such activities take place and, as we have seen, parents also have unprecedented means by which to monitor children's location. Because of this, the ways in which children experience life beyond the home have changed to a significant degree.

4.5 Not Going Out

We may often think of childhood as a time of freedom, characterised maybe by the thought of children going out to play. Such an idea, however, seems to be out of step with the experiences of contemporary children (Sutterby 2009; Tovey 2007). Although the authors may recall spending school holidays playing out with friends, leaving the house after breakfast and often not returning whilst tea-time, many younger readers would not recognise this at all. Children's books and stories may be populated by free-spirited and independent children, but if a consideration of the extent to which children are free to roam unsupervised illustrates that, this has significantly reduced over the last 75 years.

Consider the somewhat banal experience of going to school. Shaw et al. (2013) demonstrate the decline in children travelling to school without adult supervision. In the UK in 1971, 80% of seven- and eight-year olds travelled to school without an adult. But by 2006, the figure had dropped to only 12% of seven- to ten-year olds. Almost every 11-year old walked to school without adult supervision in the seventies, but now only 55% do so. In the UK, only 25% of primary school pupils travel home alone as opposed to 86% in 1971 and 76% in Germany currently. One reason given for this decline is that of safety (Bugler 2018). As road traffic has increased, so parents have been less willing to allow their children to walk, unaccompanied, to school. The paradox is that those parents who turn to driving their children to school add to the problem of increased road traffic. It is pertinent to note, however, that although walking to school has decreased, this does not mean that children do not walk (Horton et al. 2014). How children walk, however, is something that is subject to parental power (Carver et al. 2013). For Carver et al. (2013), children in their study, aged 10–12, were seen as being able to walk as a consequence of parents granting them licence to do so with such licences taking geographical features such as roads into account. Not all children, however, get licensed; the long-standing fear of child abduction (Foyster 2013; Gallagher 2008) is often something that leads to parents restricting their child's activities (Tovey 2007).

Malone (2007) writes about the experiences of middle-class children in Australia, referring to a generation that is being wrapped in bubble-wrap by over-protective parents and arguing that this restricts the ability of children to operate in society effectively. Having argued in Chapter 2 that children need a range of experiences so that they may develop resilience, it can be seen that children may lack the opportunities to develop resilience because of the way in which parents restrict their lives. Others, such as Guldberg (2009), Furedi (2008), and Jenkins (2006), have demonstrated similar concerns with parenting in respect to parents who wrap their children up, metaphorically, in cotton wool, arguing that this has a detrimental effect upon their development. This is not just a matter of the provision and use of extensive safety equipment for children taking part in activities which have come to be seen as dangerous and fraught with risk such as riding a scooter.

The reduction in unsupervised time experienced by children has the effect of increasing the influence of parents, and the impact that parents have on children's lives. As children have become subject to increasing restrictions upon when and where they may go, or be, unsupervised, so there has been a corresponding increase in time being spent either indoors or supervised. In part, Malone (2007) suggests that this is because of ideas about childhood innocence, and the corresponding idea that children should be protected from contemporary evils. With this in mind though, it is pertinent to note that although parents may see other children as a risk to their own children, they tend to ignore the fact that their own children could similarly be seen to present a risk to other children by other parents. Although there may well be evidence of a growing concern regarding childhood and innocence, a more convincing explanation for the way in which children are restricted is the emergence of a concern with risk (Crawford et al. 2017; Francis et al. 2017; Foster et al. 2014).

4.6 Children in a Changing Landscape

In one sense then, two powerful drivers acting to restrict children's activities can be identified. One is rooted in parent's self-reflection on what it means to be a good parent, especially what it would mean for them should any harm come to their children. The other is because of the way in which parents are said to see children as an emotional investment (Gillis 2009). Gillis illustrates how before legislation which both removed children from the workplace and which introduced compulsory education, and at a time when childhood mortality was high, children could be seen as an economic investment. As an economic investment though, children inevitably lived their lives within the public sphere. As children became increasingly removed from the workplace and started to move from work to school, their involvement within the public sphere was reduced and they came to be seen as a natural part of the private sphere.

Typically then, it is common to see the argument that alongside the decline in children as workers, as children became healthier and more likely to live longer, they were transformed from economic investments to emotional investments. In some ways, this reflects the arguments encompassed within the classic text by Aries (1962), the idea that childhood did not exist until quite recently partly because of high child mortality rates and partly because of the need for children to work. Heywood (2018), however, illustrates why the idea of uncaring, or uninvested, parents should be taken with some caution. Child mortality may have been significantly higher in those centuries before the twentieth century, but that is not to say that parents had no concern for their children then.

It does appear to be the case that in terms of parent–child interactions, parents appear more loving, and more emotional than has been evident previously, certainly within living memory, and at least in terms of their public personas. It is not uncommon now to hear parents and older children referring to each other as best friends. We would urge some caution though in seeing the shift from economic investment to being emotional investment as self-evident. Legislation removing children from the workplace together with compulsory education in England began in the nineteenth century. The year 1947 saw the school-leaving age raised to 15 with a further rise to 16 in 1972. If childhood is determined as being under the age of 18, it becomes obvious that children worked throughout the twentieth century. It should also be considered that the emotionally laden parenting which seems common now is something many adults over the age of 40 would not recognise. We are not saying that parents did not care for their children previously, but we are saying that parenting was different and was perhaps not as emotionally expressive as it is now.

At the same time, although parents appear more emotionally expressive within contemporary society, the extent to which they are emotionally involved may be questioned. There are a number of distractions which may interfere with parent–child interactions. Radesky et al. (2015) demonstrate how a television reduces the extent of parent–child interactions before considering the growth of mobile phone use. Parent's use of mobile phones during parent–child interactions illustrates how parents may be emotionally absent whilst being physically present. We would ask readers to observe parents with children in social places and to note just how often parents are interacting with mobile technologies rather than their children. Kildare and Middlemiss (2017) provide an extensive survey of research which demonstrates that, for many parents, mobile devices often take precedence over interacting with their children, something which the German Lifeguard Association sees as contributing to the rise in drownings (Connely 2018). We often hear that many parents would do anything for their children, but that may not extend to turning off their phone.

The emotional concerns with respect to children can also be seen in arguments that suggest that individuals have a 'right' to have children (Warnock 2004). Claims about such rights can be seen to be strategic claims which draw upon contemporary meanings regarding what family means (Barbalet 1998). In this way, the outward expression of emotions may reflect individual concerns. A significant emotional intensity can be seen in arguments about the provision of fertility treatment for couples having difficulties conceiving but it may also be seen in cases where parents are reluctant to accept the advice of medical experts regarding the provision of continuing treatment for their terminally ill children. In recent cases of this sort in England, parents have mobilised significant public support via social and national media for their children, contesting the expertise of medical staff. As such, although we would argue that many parents appear to be much more emotional in how they interact with children, emotions may also be drawn upon to achieve particular, personal, ends. In such cases, parents have often invoked arguments about the potential of their children to achieve, reinforcing the view of children as becomings.

At the same time, although it can be argued that emotions play a part in shaping how we understand what a family is, and how families should interact, this is, to some extent, determined by adult views. We should recognise that for many children today, middle-class children in particular, they have little or no free time in which they can choose how to spend it for themselves. Their lives are crammed with organised activities (Vincent and Maxwell 2016). Leverett (2011) refers to the ways in which pre-teen children are becoming domesticated as their opportunities to spend time with others away from the home is being subject to regulation and surveillance. Importantly, he argues that this domestication changes the social position of children and reinforces ideas about both their vulnerability and dependency. By confining our children to the home, the opportunities that children have to forge their own identities in the company of other children, free from supervision are significantly reduced.

Confining children to the home may seem to be a natural and reasonable approach to parenting and/or caring for children where clear boundaries between the private sphere of the home and the public sphere of commercial, industrial and social spaces are evident, but contemporary information and communication technologies, and children's access to them, have meant that these boundaries have become less certain, less clear. There was a time when a child might have been sent to their bedroom as a punishment, but that rested upon the idea of being isolated, for many children in the UK now, the bedroom is a primary location. For many children in twenty-first-century Britain, bedrooms are warm, comfortable, and are not shared. This contributes to the ways in which children are becoming more likely to be located in virtual spaces rather than real ones. As this happens though children may be faced with different types of risk (George and Odgers 2015; Hamilton-Giachritsis et al. 2013; Whittle et al. 2013). So, the actions of parents in restricting children's access to physical spaces beyond the home, ostensibly on the grounds of risk, may simply see children faced with other, different risks as a consequence of technologies which create virtual spaces. Parents may be seen as responding to the obvious threats of the physical world but are much less certain about threats within the virtual world.

From a social position, however, this may have certain positive outcomes. Recent research has suggested that reduced teenage pregnancy and drink and drug use amongst teenagers were down to children/teenagers spending more time with family in the home and using social media rather than real contact to maintain friendships (BPAS 2018). In this sense, childhood has been tamed in what could be argued is a positive way. This should be considered alongside an increasing fall in the opportunities that are available with respect to learning how to behave in a range of social settings. At one time, children used to occupy all spaces, public, private, work, and social. Now children are more restricted, they are expected to be in the home or in school or in organised activities. They are increasingly restricted in terms of the work place. They are often excluded from being in social spaces unless supervised by parents.

The result is a taming of childhood which contributes to a lack of opportunities to learn how to behave in certain spaces until they are much older. As an example, consider how a social concern about alcohol consumption has led to the widespread use of pubs requiring under-25s to carry proof of age. It was the case that under-18s did enter pubs and did drink alcohol before this practice was adopted (we also admit to doing it ourselves), but we would also point to the ways in which the behaviour of young people in pubs was mediated to a significant extent by both the adults in those pubs, and by young people themselves in not wanting to draw attention to their (illegal) behaviour. We would also suggest that enforcing legislation to keep some young people out of pubs has not stopped the underage drinking of alcohol; it has simply displaced it to far more risky locations.

In one sense, pubs and the issue of drinking illustrate the confused and contradictory landscape that children grow up in. Changes to licensing laws in the 1980s have seen a significant growth in pubs which actually cater for children. The provision of playrooms, playing equipment, colouring books, and tailored menus indicates how the accommodation of children has been adopted as a major strategy by pub chains. What this does is to normalise drinking in pubs as part of family life. Paradoxically though, when children get to an age when they are looking to be independent of the family, pubs restrict entry strictly.

In this way, another public sphere is closed off to young people at the point that they are trying to develop into adulthood.

4.7 Conclusion

So, in concluding, we can think about the ways in which childhood is tied to the family and home, but it is important to note that that this is accompanied by particular ways of understanding space, especially in terms of how children access space and what we see as appropriate spaces. In doing so, what we see is that in contemporary society, children's spaces are very often designed and monitored by adults for children. It is also the case, however, that our understanding of what is appropriate regarding how children inhabit spaces shapes how we understand children. Once again, we see that there is nothing natural about childhood; it is something that is socially constructed and is something that is open to be being tamed.

References

Aries, P. 1962. *Centuries of Childhood: A Social History of Family Life*. New York, NY: Vintage Books.

Barbalet, J. M. 1998. *Emotion, Social Theory & Social Structure: Towards a Macrosociological Approach*. Cambridge: Cambridge University Press.

Bond, E. 2010. Managing Mobile Relationships: Children's Perceptions of the Impact of the Mobile Phone on Relationships in Their Everyday Lives. In: *Childhood-Copenhagen Then London-Munksgaard Then Sage*. Denmark: Sage.

Bond, E. 2013. Mobile Phones, Risk and Responsibility: Understanding Children's Perceptions. *Cyberpsychology*, 7, Article 3.

BPAS. 2018. *Social Media, SRE, and Sensible Drinking: Understanding the Dramatic Decline in Teenage Pregnancy*. Stratford: British Pregnancy Advisory Service.

Bridges, D. 2010. Government's Construction of the Relation Between Parents and Schools in the Upbringing of Children in England: 1963–2009. *Educational Theory*, 60, 299–324.

Bristow, J. 2014. The Double Bind of Parenting Culture: Helicopter Parents and Cotton Wool Kids. In: Lee, E., Bristow, J., Faircloth, C., & Macvarish, J. (eds.), *Parenting Culture Studies*. New York, NY: Palgrave Macmillan.

Brownlie, J., & Anderson, S. 2006. "Beyond Anti-smacking": Rethinking Parent–Child Relations. *Childhood: A Global Journal of Child Research*, 13, 479–498.

Bugler, T. 2018. Parents' Fears Stop Children Cycling or Walking to School. *The Times*.

Cameron, D. 2011. Troubled Families Speech. In: Cabinet Office (ed.). London.

Carver, A., Watson, B., Shaw, B., & Hillman, M. 2013. A Comparison Study of Children's Independent Mobility in England and Australia. *Children's Geographies*, 11, 461–475.

Children's Commissioner. 2013. *A Child Rights Impact Assessment of the Anti-social Behaviour, Crime and Policing Bill* (Parts 1–6, 9).

Cockcroft, T., Bryant, R., & Keval, H. 2016. The Impact of Dispersal Powers on Congregating Youth. *Safer Communities*, 15, 213–222.

Connely, K. 2018. Child Drownings in Germany Linked to Parents' Phone 'Fixation'. *The Guardian*.

Corby, F. H. 2015. Parenting Support: How Failing Parents Understand the Experience. *Journal of Education & Social Policy*, 2(8), 11–24.

Crawford, A. 2009. Criminalizing Sociability Through Anti-social Behaviour Legislation: Dispersal Powers, Young People and the Police. *Youth Justice*, 9, 5–26.

Crawford, A., & Lister, S. 2008. Young People, Police and Dispersal Powers. *Safer Communities*, 7, 4–7. April 1.

Crawford, S. B., Bennetts, S. K., Hackworth, N. J., Cooldin, A. R., Nicholson, J. M., Green, J., Graesser, H., Matthews, J., D'esposito, F., Strazdins, L., & Zubrick, S. R. 2017. Worries, 'Weirdos', Neighborhoods and Knowing People: A Qualitative Study with Children and Parents Regarding Children's Independent Mobility. *Health & Place*, 45, 131–139.

De Magalhaes, C., & Trigo, S. F. 2017. Contracting Out Publicness: The Private Management of the Urban Public Realm and Its Implications. *Progress in Planning*, 115, 1–28.

Fingerman, K. L., Cheng, Y.-P., Wesselmann, E. D., Zarit, S., Furstenberg, F., & Birditt, K. S. 2012. Helicopter Parents and Landing Pad Kids: Intense Parental Support of Grown Children. *Journal of Marriage & Family*, 74, 880–896.

Foster, S., Villanueva, K., Wood, L., Christian, H., & Giles-Corti, B. 2014. The Impact of Parents' Fear of Strangers and Perceptions of Informal Social Control on Children's Independent Mobility. *Health & Place*, 26, 60–68.

Foyster, E. 2013. The 'New World of Children' Reconsidered: Child Abduction in Late Eighteenth- and Early Nineteenth-Century England. *Journal of British Studies*, 52, 669–692.

Francis, J., Martin, K., Wood, L., & Foster, S. 2017. 'I'll Be Driving You to School for the Rest of Your Life': A Qualitative Study of Parents' Fear of Stranger Danger. *Journal of Environmental Psychology*, 53, 112–120.

Freeman, M., & Saunders, B. J. 2014. Can We Conquer Child Abuse If We Don't Outlaw Physical Chastisement of Children? *International Journal of Children's Rights*, 22, 681–709.

Furedi, F. 2008. *Paranoid Parenting: Why Ignoring the Experts May Be Best for Your Child*. London: Bloomsbury.

Gallagher, B. 2008. Fear of the Unknown. *Safer Communities*, 7, 22–25. July 1.

Garrett, P. M. 2009. *'Transforming' Children's Services? Social Work, Neoliberalism and the 'Modern' World*. Maidenhead, UK: Open University Press.

Garrett, P. B. 2018. *Welfare Words: Critical Social Work & Social Policy*. London: Sage.

George, M., & Odgers, C. 2015. Seven Fears and the Science of How Mobile Technologies May Be Influencing Adolescents in the Digital Age. *Perspectives on Psychological Science: A Journal of the Association for Psychological Science*, 10, 832–851.

Gillis, J. 2009. Transitions to Modernity. In: Qvortrup, J., Corsaro, W. A., & Honig, M.-S. (eds.), *The Palgrave Handbook of Childhood Studies*. London: Palgrave.

Guldberg, H. 2009. *Reclaiming Childhood: Freedom and Play in an Age of Fear*. London: Routledge.

Hamilton-Giachritsis, C., Whittle, H., Beech, A., & Collings, G. 2013. A Review of Online Grooming: Characteristics and Concerns. *Aggression and Violent Behavior*, 18, 62–70.

Hasinoff, A. A. 2017. Where Are You? Location Tracking and the Promise of Child Safety. *Television & New Media*, 18, 496–512.

Heywood, C. 2018. *A History of Childhood*. Cambridge: Polity Press.

Horton, J., Christensen, P., Kraftl, P., & Hadfield-Hill, S. 2014. 'Walking … Just Walking': How Children and Young People's Everyday Pedestrian Practices Matter. *Social & Cultural Geography*, 15, 94–115.

Jenkins, N. E. 2006. 'You Can't Wrap Them Up in Cotton Wool!' Constructing Risk in Young People's Access to Outdoor Play. *Health, Risk & Society*, 8, 379–393.

Johnstone, C. 2016. After the Asbo: Extending Control Over Young People's Use of Public Space in England and Wales. *Critical Social Policy*, 36, 716–726.

Kildare, C. A., & Middlemiss, W. 2017. Impact of Parents Mobile Device Use on Parent–Child Interaction: A Literature Review. *Computers in Human Behavior*, 75, 579–593.

Kish, A. M., & Newcombe, P. A. 2015. "Smacking Never Hurt Me!" Identifying Myths Surrounding the Use of Corporal Punishment. *Personality and Individual Differences*, 87, 121–129.

Lemoyne, T., & Buchanan, T. 2011. Does 'Hovering' Matter? Helicopter Parenting and Its Effect on Well-Being. *Sociological Spectrum*, 31, 399–418.

Leverett, S. 2011. Children's Spaces. In: Foley, P., & Leverett, S. (eds.), *Children and Young Peoples Spaces: Developing Practice*. Basingstoke: Palgrave Macmillan.

Lewis, J. 2011. Parenting Programmes in England: Policy Development and Implementation Issues, 2005–2010. *Journal of Social Welfare & Family Law*, 33, 107–121.

Malone, K. 2007. The Bubble-Wrap Generation: Children Growing Up in Walled Gardens. *Environmental Education Research*, 13, 513–527.

Marano, H. E. 2004. A Nation of Wimps. *Psychology Today*.

Padilla-Walker, L. M., & Nelson, L. J. 2012. Black Hawk Down? Establishing Helicopter Parenting as a Distinct Construct from Other Forms of Parental Control During Emerging Adulthood. *Journal of Adolescence*, 35, 1117–1190.

Pain, R. 2006. Paranoid Parenting? Rematerializing Risk and Fear for Children. *Social & Cultural Geography*, 7, 221–243.

Peluchette, J. V. E., Kovanic, N., & Partridge, D. 2013. Helicopter Parents Hovering in the Workplace: What Should HR Managers Do? *Business Horizons*, 56, 601–609.

Perry, N. B., Dollar, J. M., Calkins, S. D., Keane, S. P., & Shanahan, L. 2018. Childhood Self-Regulation as a Mechanism Through Which Early Overcontrolling Parenting Is Associated with Adjustment in Preadolescence. *Developmental Psychology*, 54, 1542–1555.

Radesky, J., Miller, A. L., Rosenblum, K. L., Appugliese, D., Kaciroti, N., & Lumeng, J. C. 2015. Maternal Mobile Device Use During a Structured Parent–Child Interaction Task. *Academic Pediatrics*, 15, 238–244.

Romagnoli, A., & Wall, G. 2012. 'I know I'm a Good Mom': Young, Low-Income Mothers' Experiences with Risk Perception, Intensive Parenting Ideology and Parenting Education Programmes. *Health, Risk & Society*, 14, 273–289.

Sayer, T. 2008. *Critical Practice in Working with Children*. Basingstoke, NY: Palgrave Macmillan.

Schiffrin, H., Godfrey, H., Liss, M., & Erchull, M. 2015. Intensive Parenting: Does It Have the Desired Impact on Child Outcomes? *Journal of Child & Family Studies*, 24, 2322–2331.

Shaw, B., Watson, B., Frauendienst, B., Redecker, A., Jones, T., & Hillman, M. 2013. *Children's Independent Mobility: A Comparative Study in England and Germany (1971–2010)*. London: Policy Studies Institute.

Simpson, B. 2014. Tracking Children, Constructing Fear: GPS and the Manufacture of Family Safety. *Information and Communications Technology Law*, 23, 273–285.

Smith, K. M. 2014. *The Government of Childhood: Discourse, Power and Subjectivity*. Basingstoke: Palgrave Macmillan.

Stearns, P. N. 2003. *Anxious Parents: A History of Modern Childrearing in America*. New York: New York University Press.

Stern, J. 2014. *Loneliness and Solitude in Education: How to Value Individuality and Create an Enstatic School*. Oxford and New York: Peter Lang.

Sutterby, J. A. 2009. What Kids Don't Get to Do Anymore and Why. *Childhood Education*, 85, 289–292.

Tovey, H. 2007. *Playing Outdoors: Spaces and Places, Risk and Challenge*. Maidenhead: McGraw-Hill and Open University Press.

Van Ingen, D. J., Freiheit, S. R., Steinfeldt, J. A., Moore, L. L., Wimer, D. J., Knutt, A. D., Scapinello, S., & Roberts, A. 2015. Helicopter Parenting: The Effect of an Overbearing Caregiving Style on Peer Attachment and Self-Efficacy. *Journal of College Counseling*, 18, 7–20.

Veltkamp, G., & Brown, P. 2017. The Everyday Risk Work of Dutch Child-Healthcare Professionals: Inferring 'Safe' and 'Good' Parenting Through Trust, as Mediated by a Lens of Gender and Class. *Sociology of Health & Illness*, 39, 1297–1313.

Vincent, C. 2017. "The Children Have Only Got One Education and You Have to Make Sure It's a Good One": Parenting and Parent–School Relations in a Neoliberal Age. *Gender and Education*, 29, 541–557.

Vincent, C., & Maxwell, C. 2016. Parenting Priorities and Pressures: Furthering Understanding of 'Concerted Cultivation'. *Discourse: Studies in the Cultural Politics of Education*, 37, 269–281.

Vota, N. 2017. Keeping the Free-Range Parent Immune from Child Neglect: You Cannot Tell Me How to Raise My Children. *Family Court Review*, 55, 152–167.

Warnock, M. 2004. *Making Babies: Is There a Right to Have Children?* Oxford: Oxford University Press.

Whittle, H., Hamilton-Giachritsis, C., Beech, A., & Collings, G. 2013. A Review of Young People's Vulnerabilities to Online Grooming. *Aggression and Violent Behavior*, 18, 135–146.

Zhang, X. 2017. Identifying Consumerist Privately Owned Public Spaces: The Ideal Type of Mass Private Property. *Urban Studies*, 54, 3464–3479.

5

Taming in the Early Years

Abstract The Early Years has been a major site for State **intervention** and regulation. It can be argued that policy agendas such as Every Child Matters represent ways in which the State colonises and regulates or governs childhood. For the State, it is concerns with education, work, and **safeguarding** which have dominated policy approaches and have contributed to the taming of childhood. Children's status as becomings is epitomised in the way in which **play** has been replaced by a focus on education and concerns about school **readiness**, an approach which can be understood as **schoolification**. This operates alongside a concern with **vulnerability** and safeguarding wherein risk is something to be managed.

Keywords Intervention · Safeguarding · Play · Readiness · Schoolification · Vulnerability

5.1 Introduction

Chapter 4 considered the home environment and the actions of parents in respect of the taming of childhood. In this chapter, we focus on the early years on the grounds that this represents the first category of childhood that is subject to intervention and support that is external to the home and family. As a term, the early years could be said to have little meaning within the family, but it does become meaningful when viewed in terms of a policy agenda and in terms of provision. In considering childhood then, a consideration of the early years can be recognised as both a life stage and a form of practice within a policy context. In terms of the taming of childhood, the issue of vulnerability or of dependency, as considered in Chapter 2, may appear as obvious and this can distract from the idea of taming. What will be argued in this chapter is that in recent decades in particular, the early years have come under increased scrutiny and have been subject to greater State intervention than was ever the case. So, where Chapter 4 was concerned with the influence of family and the place of children within the home, this chapter considers the influence on taming that is a consequence of children, and childhood, being seen as a matter for policy. As such, this focus and intervention can be seen as setting the foundations for taming. It will be argued that the lived experiences of the early years have changed in recent decades as a consequence of State actions which have a particular purpose. Following from this, we frame our discussion on education, future work, and safeguarding as key examples.

As a part of childhood, the notion of the early years has become firmly established within the UK. This is reinforced by government policies which have brought the early years to the fore such as the development of the Birth to Three matters framework (Langston and Abbott 2004). This can be said to have shaped the Early Years Foundation Stage (introduced in 2008, revised in 2012) and the Early Years Professional Status (EYPS). The EYPS was introduced in 2007 and reviewed in 2012. The aims of these policy developments illustrate a particular focus that was brought to bear upon the early years during the time of the New Labour governments (1997–2010). Alongside an understanding of the early years as being a foundational time within the life-course, there was also a concern to enhance practice within Early Years settings by upskilling and professionalising the workforce. The EYPS was one aspect of the strategy by which this would be achieved. Underpinning this is a view of children as becomings wherein the early years is considered to be vital. It is a view of childhood as being comprised of building blocks with the early years as the foundation for later life.

What is evident in these developments though is a shift in focus with respect to young children, within which concerns about care and play come to be seen as having less value. This takes place alongside a corresponding emphasis on formal education coming to the fore. This shift, however, can be seen to rest upon distinguishing play from education. In making this distinction, play, especially child-directed play, is presented as of little value when compared to a form of education that is structured and directed for children. As a consequence of this emphasis upon formal education, greater levels of concern are also placed upon formal settings. Because of this shift away from informal play, the care and education of children being undertaken outside of the home become expected and more scrutiny is given to those who will provide it.

Prior to the twenty-first century, the idea of studying Early Years or Early Childhood to degree level was rarely an option and most practitioners would only have been expected to be qualified to level 3 (of the national qualifications framework) through following a BTEC, Diploma in Nursery Nursing, or National Nursery Examination Board (NNEB) qualification (the NNEB became Cache after merging with the Council for Early Years Awards in 1994), if they were qualified at all. It was usual that those working in early years settings would have been referred to as Nursery Nurses with its obvious emphasis upon the importance of health, something that is reiterated in the position of Health Visiting. The establishment of Health Visitors ostensibly indicates social concerns regarding the care and parenting of very young children and it remains the case that Health Visitors still have a significant role with respect to early years as is evident in the revised Healthy Child Programme (Underdown and Barlow 2012; DoH 2009) and the planned expansion of Health Visiting by the Coalition Government (2010–2015) (DoH 2011). The extent to which this is driven by a concern with care, however, is debatable and it can be argued that there is a greater concern regarding early intervention which, in turn, positions Health Visiting as surveillance.

It could be said that, traditionally, pre-school children were seen as somewhat unproblematic. Their place was within the home, within their family, and an understanding of potential problems tended to be limited to health matters. In one sense, they were waiting to start school, usually just before their fifth birthday. The focus was on providing care, but this care was a private matter and there was no real sense of education starting before the child started formal schooling. For infants, health was the primary concern alongside the opportunity to play and develop social skills. Because the under-fives were expected to be within the home, their care was generally seen as a matter of parenting, even though there was some recognition that it was sometimes necessary to try to change how some parents parented.

This chapter then is concerned with the way in which young children have come to be located in a different social position. It is concerned with how they have come to be the focus of the State and how, as this has happened, they have become subject to much broader concerns about their development than was once the case. We consider that these developments have resulted in a taming of the early years which can be seen to have had an impact on children, parents, and practitioners and, in doing so, has limited the opportunities for the early years.

5.2 The Growing Role of the State

Part of the reason for the growing involvement of the State may be seen as being a consequence of changing work patterns. Paradoxically though, it is the actions of the State in terms of economic deregulation which has done much to change working patterns and which in turn has impacted upon the capacity of parents to parent. This is particularly relevant with respect to women and work. When considering the introduction of policies which came to be referred to as the Welfare State at the end of the 1940s, it is evident that this reflected a society where married women were expected to remain within the home. Whilst this was only really relevant for some women, UK society has moved to a position where the majority of women are now expected to go out to work. Because of this change, there is an inevitable consequence for the care of children, something which Williams (2004) has referred to as a caring gap. It seems important to note that we are not claiming that women have only just started going out to work. In spite of the mythical idea of some golden age of the family in which men were the breadwinner and women the homemaker, women have always worked. Women from low socio-economic groups in particular have always worked, often because for some men, the idea of a family wage, a wage sufficient for a man to support his family, was always a little out of reach, sometimes because of other factors such as being widowed or because of divorce. The 1980s, however, saw the start of other changes which have changed the way adults in families work (Rönkä et al. 2017; Hegewisch and Gornick 2011; Vincent and Neis 2011).

Political developments during the 1980s, influenced by neoliberalism, have had a significant impact upon the economy, which, in turn, has impacted upon the family. Deindustrialisation changed the position of many men within families which, in turn, increased the pressure on women within families to secure paid employment. At the same time, the deregulation of existing practices, such as extended retail opening hours or the development of new kinds of work such as the rise of customer service centres amongst other things, has led to an increased demand for many workers to be at work in the evening, during the night, and at weekends. This has an inevitable impact upon family life. When considered alongside rising housing costs, it becomes understandable as to why there has been a decrease in the single-household wage earner, in which it was usually the woman who stayed at home. Paradoxically, the development and extension of welfare and caring work also contributed to this change, as these jobs tended to be staffed by women.

The consequence is that, in contemporary UK society, it has become quite normal for infants, the early years, to be cared for outside of the home. The introduction of free nursery care within the UK is not in itself a new phenomenon (West and Noden 2016), but the policies introduced by the Labour governments (1997–2010) saw a range of polices aimed at parents and families (Smith 2013). This has contributed to normalising the practice of children going to nursery with policies such as the provision of funding 2-year olds acting as a means to enable women on low incomes to access training or work (Gibb et al. 2011). Such developments contribute to a changed pattern of childcare when compared to previous generations (notwithstanding the extensive provision of nursery places during the Second World War). The care of the early years is often complex though, and children within the UK are very likely to spend part of their days being cared for by friends and family as well as by paid staff.

So, as a consequence of social changes that have been brought about by the deregulation of labour markets and the workplace, policies that are rooted within neoliberal politics, we can see a societal shift. It is this shift which creates the preconditions for the increased regulation of children. This reflects Foucault's concerns regarding how the State comes to take an interest in the population (Wells 2018) and facilitates what Smith (2014) refers to as the government of childhood. In part, this also reflects the ways in which the State sees children as becomings, whether that be becoming workers, citizens, taxpayers, or even problems. Because of this, it can be argued that the State sees children as existing within a process, that is, the process towards becoming an adult. In this way, state interventions may be seen as attempts to exert some control over that process so as to produce outcomes which the State sees as desirable. As part of this, we can consider how this increases pressures on parents to place their children in the hands of paid staff and how parents become drawn into a discourse of potential and readiness with respect to becoming.

The precursor to governmental frameworks such as the EYFS can be seen as Every Child Matters (ECM) (DfES 2004) often seen as being precipitated by the Victoria Climbie' case. ECM was important in how it established the value and importance of early intervention (Knowles 2009). The idea of early intervention not only reflects concerns to deal with problems when they first arise, it also illustrates a concern with the ways in which early childhood experiences are said to influence later life. For example, studies which show how young children from poor backgrounds start from a position of disadvantage and fail to make up ground later on (Morrissey and Vinopal 2018).

With respect to both Every Child Matters and the Children Act (2004), the Labour governments from 1997 to 2010 emphasised the place of children within society, though this was generally driven by a view of children's future role (Lister 2005). One key aspect of Labour's approach towards children was SureStart, which led to the widespread introduction of Children's centres across the UK. Although popular and effective (Donetto and Maben 2015; Hall et al. 2015; Lewis et al. 2011; Anning and Ball 2008), the policies introduced by the Coalition and Conservative governments since 2010 have seen the dismantling of such services. It can be seen that the introduction of SureStart owed much to the conceptual ideas of Bronfenbrenner (1979), and the introduction of HeadStart within the USA. Bronfenbrenner's ideas are often reduced to a model of childhood that is represented as concentric circles with the child at the centre. In this way, it is shown that the child exists within a framework of influences emanating out from the immediate family through the school, the community, and society. As such, the child's lived world cannot be understood without considering the political context of any given society. This is because it is the political context which shapes the public services that are provided with respect to children.

As a policy, SureStart can be seen to operate on different levels. Although ostensibly aimed at children, especially in terms of preparing children for school, SureStart also acted in ways which encouraged and supported women into the workplace (Smith 2013). This was consistent with New Labour's approach of seeing adults primarily as workers, rather than as parents. What this also reflects, however, is the ways in which the view of children as becomings is reinforced in a way which promotes the idea of readiness (MacBlain et al. 2017; Iorio and Parnell 2015). This firmly reinforces the idea of children as becomings within an understanding of childhood as a process, though we can also see how a discourse of readiness conflicts with the way in which the Early Years Foundation Stage establishes a discourse which positions each child as unique (Brooks and Murray 2018). We would argue that in such a conflict, the uniqueness of individual children always seems to lose out, that there is a greater pressure to view children as homogenous.

5.3 Towards Education

Policy approaches in relation to childhood generally reflect ideas in which children are understood as being located within a particular stage of development and how this makes some things acceptable and others not acceptable. For example, in relation to work, it is not to say that children should never work or that they do not work; only that work is not generally accepted as being appropriate whilst they are children. As such, it is considered that for children, work should not inhibit their opportunity to engage with education. In practice, this is not as straightforward as some types of work are allowed. Consider also that children who provide caring work within the home are very often overlooked in concerns about work. With respect to many policies regarding childhood, we would argue that it is an idealised, middle-class version of childhood which predominates. This idealised version, however, obscures the reality of many children's lives in terms of drudgery, abuse, homelessness, and caring responsibilities. What is evident though is that although the idea of children as workers within the present is seen as unacceptable, the idea of children as future workers is often firmly embedded within social policies, even those that are aimed at very young children.

This can be seen in the Ofsted (2017) report Bold Beginnings. As an Ofsted publication, it is the case that this report carries with it significant weight and it is likely to have influence with respect to the educational experiences of children in the early years, especially the reception year. It is noted, however, that it is a report which draws on a somewhat small number of schools, and on schools that are categorised as being good. What can be seen though is that Bold Beginnings contributes to concepts that we have previously raised as being somewhat contentious, namely, "school readiness" and "schoolification" (Dubiel and Kilner 2017; Neaum 2016).

Critics of Bold Beginnings have pointed to the way in which it adopts a formalised view of teaching alongside an understanding of the Reception Year as existing to prepare children for Key Stage 1 (TACTYC 2017). In this way, Bold Beginnings contributes to the tensions that can be seen between approaches to teaching in the early years which recognise the importance of play, and those which advocate a formal curriculum. In spite of the young age that children start school in the UK when compared with other European countries (Murray 2017), the early years had tended to be left out of discussions about education and especially about work. That can be seen to have changed within recent decades, especially since the introduction of the EYFS. This has created a much more intensive experience of schooling at all ages than was once the case with significant emphasis being placed on attendance. As a consequence of this, parents within the UK may be fined for taking their children out of school for the purposes of taking a holiday and children are under pressure with respect to school attendance when they are at a life stage that means they can be ill a lot.

In considering these developments regarding education, Dahlberg (2011) draws attention to the underpinning ideas which shape provision for children in the early years. She does this by contrasting the *pre-primary* approach with the *social pedagogic* approach (italics in original). She notes that the pre-primary approach, as found within the UK, "is normally teacher-directed and children's performance is often benchmarked and assessed via prescribed targets generally pertaining to cognitive development" (p. 229). This is significantly different compared to how pre-school was once referred to as playschool. Where the focus was once on play and socialisation, this has now been replaced by a focus on preparation for learning (Stirrup et al. 2017a, b).

The emphasis upon early years provision being focused on education is made clear in the government document, Statutory framework for the early years foundation stage: setting the standards for learning, development and care for children from birth to five (DfE 2017). This provides a regulatory framework which

> defines what providers must do, working in partnership with parents and/or carers, to promote the learning and development of all children in their care, and to ensure they are ready for school. The learning and development requirements are informed by the best available evidence on how children learn and reflect the broad range of skills, knowledge and attitudes children need as foundations for good future progress.

Early years providers must guide the development of children's capabilities with a view to ensuring that children in their care complete the EYFS ready to benefit fully from the opportunities ahead of them. (p. 7)

The view of children as becomings is clearly embedded within this framework. It is also strongly associated with the idea of school-readiness (Brooks and Murray 2018; Murray 2017; Stirrup et al. 2017b; Neaum 2016). For Stirrup et al. (2017b), a general concern with accountability intersects with the idea of being school-ready to shape a particular experience within early years settings, an experience which they argue is also mediated by ideas about social class. In part, this is shaped by how children from different class backgrounds are seen, something which is manifest as assumptions about the nature of children when they first enter early years settings. With social differences in mind, it can be seen how funding initiatives for the early years are based upon the premise that children from poorer households are starting from a deficit position.

5.4 Readiness for School, or to Work?

The SureStart model discussed above was originally intended to improve outcomes for children from poor or disadvantaged backgrounds. This is something which fits easily with a discourse of childhood as a process and children as becomings. Although SureStart and the subsequent model of Children's Centres have much that can be commended (Miller and Hevey 2012; NESS 2012; Frost and Parton 2009; Barnes et al. 2007), this also reflects and reinforces the colonisation of childhood by the State. It may also be seen as a reflection of Human Capital theory with respect to Early Childhood Education and Care (Campbell-Barr and Nygård 2014). As such a consideration of policy approaches such as Every Child Matters and the Children Act demonstrates further ways in which childhood comes to be viewed as something to be shaped with a view to achieving particular ends.

So, as a consequence of the policy approach that was reinforced under the 1997–2010 Labour governments, the idea of care within the early years is replaced by a concern for learning. As a consequence of this, what has come to the fore is a greater concern with establishing school or educational readiness (Evans 2016; Palmer 2009). As we indicated within Chapter 2, however, some terms may be seen as being somewhat slippery. As a way of understanding, children readiness is a very new concept. As with other concepts regarding children though, it is invariably something that is used as though it were self-evident and unproblematic. In practice, it is not a concept that is clearly defined beyond being presented as some distinguishing measure wherein some children are ready and some are not (Cavadel and Frye 2017). It seems churlish to question what is meant by school readiness, but it is not unambiguous and within a political culture which privileges accountability what counts as readiness may be both specific and limited (Falchi and Friedman 2015). In practice, it serves to increase pressure on to parents with regard to a combination of their children's behaviour and educational ability on entering school.

Overall, policy approaches such as SureStart do give greater prominence to the early years sector in one sense, in that they bestow a greater sense of importance with respect to the role of early years workers. Often though, this subsequently changes their role though from that of caring to that of preparing, as they are tasked with getting children ready for school. This reinforces a future-oriented understanding of childhood within which the early years becomes a waystation. Any discussion of readiness, however, implies juxtaposition. We would argue that readiness cannot be taken for granted. It is obvious that in focusing upon readiness, some children are deemed to be ready whilst other children are deemed to be not ready. Readiness though is generally seen as moving beyond a concern with cognitive development, in that not being ready is generally seen as having social causes (Morrissey and Vinopal 2018). As part of this understanding, some children become cast as vulnerable to not being ready.

In turn, establishing a need to be ready for school can provide a justification for State intervention when the State is able to assert that it is the nature of some parenting approaches which leads to this situation. As has been suggested previously, there is a degree of seductiveness regarding this sort of reasoning. It becomes very difficult to argue that we would not want children to be ready for school and it may be easy to accept that not all children have the same experiences. This makes social policy approaches which act upon children to become more acceptable. As a discourse of readiness becomes established, so we might see that the taming of childhood is the consequence of early years practices which are driven by policies with a specific concern. That said, it would be misleading to suggest that early years policy are dominated by concerns regarding readiness for learning. A general concern with a particular aspect of child welfare, of a sort, has been central to recent policy and practice developments and this can be seen to have had real consequences for taming.

5.5 Protecting the Early Years

There is often a sense that childhood is viewed as having inherent difficulties that can be overcome through policy approaches which act upon children, albeit sometimes tangentially (Macfarlane and Lakhani 2015; Simpson and Envy 2015). The impetus behind social concerns for children may be seen as being rooted in child mortality, and with respect to abuse from parents and carers, especially with respect to particular socio-economic or minority groups. This has led to policies and practice that attempt to protect the most vulnerable of children, though vulnerable is often erroneously seen as being synonymous with poor children.

One key issue which New Labour can be seen as being responsible for is the intensification of the idea that children are characterised by vulnerability and that this intersects with a strong concern about risk. This concern is evident within much social policy aimed at children and has been for some time (Turnbull 2016; Turnbull and Spence 2011), but a view of risk as being something to remove tends to be dominant (1992). This is evident in the way that Every Child Matters ushered in a change, from child protection to safeguarding. This is important because the move to safeguarding casts a wide net in that as a consequence not only did every child matter, but every child was at risk. It also established that everyone had a duty to safeguard children.

In this way, the move to safeguarding justifies the restrictions that may be placed upon children under the guise of keeping them safe. Risk has come to represent an unambiguous, or monolithic, threat. It has become something to manage, preferably to eradicate. The ubiquitous risk assessment procedures adopted by institutions such as nurseries and schools tend to promote ways of reducing risk rather than finding ways of accommodating and utilising it. This has had significant consequences for children's lived experiences.

Increasing concerns regarding safeguarding foreground concerns with risk and emphasise the idea of children as vulnerable. These concerns have led to significant restrictions on children's activities (Guldberg 2009; Jenkins 2006) which can be viewed as taming. One consequence of this is that childhood is increasingly tamed and this restricts not only children's lived experiences, it also restricts their opportunities for development (Harper 2017). Moss et al. (2000) illustrate how contrasting discourses of children and what they are capable of contributes to differing ways of providing for children. Within the Reggio Emilia approach, in Italy, the child is seen as intrinsically rich with the capacity for self-development. This Italian approach is contrasted with UK in which children are viewed as vulnerable, as being in need. This results in a very different childhood for the UK child.

Within the UK, the safeguarding agenda constructs the image of a world that is not only intrinsically dangerous, it is populated by dangerous individuals who pose an ever-present threat to children. As a consequence, an exaggerated focus on safety restricts children's activities in spite of any long-term detriment that this may pose to health (Wheway 2008). Alongside this, the threat from strangers and/or individuals who work with children is formalised within the Criminal Records Bureau (CRB) checks, now the Disclosure and Barring Service (DBS) which operate on the basis that anyone not in possession of a satisfactory check should be considered a threat. As was discussed in Chapter 4, one of the consequences of an over-sensitivity to risk is risk aversion with parents increasingly restricting what children can do. A similar process applies within nurseries and schools as activities become prohibited on the grounds that they may expose children to danger. As such, children's lives become increasingly tamed.

Although recent developments such as Forest Schools (Harris 2018; Harper 2017; Knight 2009; Tovey 2007) appear to be a response to the over-protection of children, such approaches also rest upon teachers not exerting unnecessary levels of supervision. The idea of children being in danger is often raised as a concern, but it is the case that children experiencing injury, or accidents leading to death, in the twenty-first century is overwhelmingly seen as tragedy and a loss for the parents. Children's activities then may be seen as having been tamed to address the needs of parents rather than to provide for children.

5.6 Conclusion

What is reinforced within these discussions is that with respect to childhood, there are a number of discourses, some of which may be seen as competing or contradictory. This is evident in the way in which a discourse of school readiness promotes development as being uniform but can be accepted alongside a discourse of each child being unique. This is but one example of our capacity to acknowledge contradictory or competing discourses. Similarly, we often hear concerns about health and safety and the ways in which these are given to justify restricting what children can do, but the emphasis is generally on safety, and health is very often overlooked. As such a discourse of childhood may often be referred to, but it would be more accurate to refer to discourses about childhood.

There is also a contemporary discourse regarding children which posits them in terms of being valued. This is manifest in a number of ways. Chapter 6 will comment upon the way in which schools often promote themselves as valuing children as individuals whilst simultaneously stifling individuality. Our concern within this chapter has considered some of the ways in which we can see the State having increasingly come to value children, although where we have previously considered parents as seeing children as emotional assets, we are minded to say that this is not the case for the State. We would suggest that, for the State, children are still seen in terms of being economic becomings.

We would also suggest that seeing children as economic becomings contributes to interventions within children's lives which have the effect of taming childhood. This is because when childhood comes to be viewed as a transitional process within which children pass through stages to attain an end-state, i.e. adulthood, so we can see that the preconditions are created for interventions which have the aim of transforming the child into a particular type of adult. Irrespective of parental involvement then we can see that this is embedded within a range of approaches that are instigated and enacted within social policies. There is a danger though that this suggests that parents are not part of those policies and we draw attention to ways in which they are; both policy-makers and those that carry out policy are often parents also. So, despite the discourse which suggests that parent are responsible for shaping early childhood, this is heavily influenced by policy as has already been suggested. The involvement of parents is always within the context of policies at any given time.

For example, Wyness (2012) uses the categories of play and work to show how this informs contemporary understanding of childhood. Using this approach, childhood comes to be viewed as the absence of responsibilities to work. In fact, this is further strengthened by legal restrictions which prohibit children from working, though this should always be considered alongside the fact that many children do work as has been established. For example, although we may immediately think about children having paper rounds or Saturday jobs, children also work as actors and models. Children also work as a consequence of caring responsibilities and in the course of schoolwork under the guise of homework.

This is pertinent to children as a whole because not only there is the tendency to see the physical and cognitive capacities of children as a justification for them not working, there are also legal restrictions which reinforce the idea that they should not work. In relation to the early years though, it may seem ludicrous to consider that such young children could ever be expected to work. This attitude perhaps conveniently forgets that historically even very young children, especially Working Class children, would have been expected to work, though once again, there was significant variation with respect to age and expectations (Heywood 2018; Wilkes 2011; Humphries 2010). What is evident, however, is that the development of legislation prohibiting, or restricting, child labour must be a response to such labour (Gillis 2009), though the ideas which have driven such developments may be more complex than a mere concern with child welfare (Hendrick 2005).

References

Anning, A., & Ball, M. 2008. *Improving Services for Young Children: From Sure Start to Children's Centres.* Los Angeles, CA and London: Sage.

Barnes, J., Belsky, J., & Melhuish, E. C. 2007. *The National Evaluation of Sure Start: Does Area-Based Early Intervention Work?* Bristol: Policy.

Beck, U. 1992. *Risk Society: Towards a New Modernity.* London: Sage.

Bronfenbrenner, U. 1979. *The Ecology of Human Development: Experiments by Nature and Design.* Cambridge, MA: Harvard University Press.

Brooks, E., & Murray, J. 2018. Ready, Steady, Learn: School Readiness and Children's Voices in English Early Childhood Settings. *Education 3–13*, 46, 143–156.

Campbell-Barr, V., & Nygård, M. 2014. Losing Sight of the Child? Human Capital Theory and Its Role for Early Childhood Education and Care Policies in Finland and England Since the Mid-1990s. *Contemporary Issues in Early Childhood*, 15, 346–359.

Cavadel, E. W., & Frye, D. A. 2017. Not Just Numeracy and Literacy: Theory of Mind Development and School Readiness Among Low-IncomeChildren. *Developmental Psychology*, 53, 2290.

Dahlberg, G. 2011. Policies in Early Childhood Education and Care: Potentialities for Agency, Play and Learning. In: Corsaro, W. A., Qvortrup, J., & Honig, M.-S. (eds.), *The Palgrave Handbook of Childhood Studies.* Basingstoke: Palgrave Macmillan.

DfE. 2017. Statutory Framework for the Early Years Foundation Stage: Setting the Standards for Learning, Development and Care for Children from Birth to Five. In: Education (ed.). London: HM Government.

DfES. 2004. *Every Child Matters: Change for Children/ Department for Education and Skills.* London: Department for Education and Skills.

DoH. 2009. *Healthy Child Programme: Pregnancy and the First Five Years of Life.* London: Department of Health.

DoH. 2011. *Health Visitor Implementation Plan 2011–2015: A Call to Action.* London: Department of Health.

Donetto, S., & Maben, J. 2015. 'These Places Are Like a Godsend': A Qualitative Analysis of Parents' Experiences of Health Visiting Outside the Home and of Children's Centres Services. *Health Expectations*, 18, 2559–2569.

Dubiel, J., & Kilner, D. 2017. *Teaching Four and Five Year Olds: The Hundred Review of the Reception Year in England.* Available http://earlyexcellence.com/wp-content/uploads/2017/05/EX_TheHundredReview_ExecutiveSummary.pdf. Accessed 22 January 2018.

Evans, K. L. 2016. *Deconstructing 'Readiness' in Early Childhood Education.* University of Exeter.

Falchi, L., & Friedman, J. W. 2015. Rethinking the Discourse of Readiness in Preschool. In: Iorio, J. M., & Parnell, W. (eds.), *Rethinking Readiness in Early Childhood Education: Implications for Policy and Practice.* New York, NY: Palgrave Macmillan.

Frost, N., & Parton, N. 2009. *Understanding Children's Social Care: Politics, Policy and Practice.* Los Angeles: Sage.

Gibb, J., Jelicic, H., & La Valle, I. 2011. *Rolling Out Free Early Education for Disadvantaged Two Year Olds: An Implementation Study for Local Authorities and Providers.* London: National Children's Bureau.

Gillis, J. 2009. Transitions to Modernity. In: Qvortrup, J., Corsaro, W. A., & Honig, M.-S. (eds.), *The Palgrave Handbook of Childhood Studies.* London: Palgrave.

Guldberg, H. 2009. *Reclaiming Childhood: Freedom and Play in an Age of Fear.* London: Routledge.

Hall, J., Eisenstadt, N., Sylva, K., Smith, T., Sammons, P., Smith, G., Evangelou, M., Goff, J., Tanner, E., Agur, M., & Hussey, D. 2015. A Review of the Services Offered by English Sure Start Children's Centres in 2011 and 2012. *Oxford Review of Education*, 41, 89–104.

Harper, N. J. 2017. Outdoor Risky Play and Healthy Child Development in the Shadow of the "Risk Society": A Forest and Nature School Perspective. *Child & Youth Services*, 38, 318–334.

Harris, F. 2018. Outdoor Learning Spaces: The Case of Forest School. *Area*, 50, 222–231.

Hegewisch, A., & Gornick, J. C. 2011. The Impact of Work-Family Policies on Women's Employment: A Review of Research from OECD Countries. *Community, Work & Family*, 14, 119–138.

Hendrick, H. 2005. Children and Social Policies. In: Hendrick, H. (ed.), *Child Welfare and Social Policy: An Essential Reader.* Bristol: Policy Press.

Heywood, C. 2018. *A History of Childhood*. Cambridge: Polity Press.
Humphries, J. 2010. *Childhood and Child Labour in the British Industrial Revolution*. Cambridge, UK and New York: Cambridge University Press.
Iorio, J. M., & Parnell, W. 2015. *Rethinking Readiness in Early Childhood Education: Implications for Policy and Practice*. Basingstoke: Palgrave Macmillan.
Jenkins, N. E. 2006. 'You Can't Wrap Them Up in Cotton Wool!' Constructing Risk in Young People's Access to Outdoor Play. *Health, Risk & Society*, 8, 379–393.
Knight, S. 2009. *Forest Schools and Outdoor Learning in the Early Years*. Los Angeles, CA and London: Sage.
Knowles, G. 2009. *Ensuring Every Child Matters*. London and Thousand Oaks, CA: Sage.
Langston, A., & Abbott, L. 2004. *Birth to Three Matters: Supporting the Framework of Effective Practice*. Maidenhead: Open University Press.
Lewis, J., Cuthbert, R., & Sarre, S. 2011. What Are Children's Centres? The Development of CC Services, 2004–2008. *Social Policy & Administration*, 45, 35–53.
Lister, R. 2005. Investing in the Citizen-Workers of the Future. In: Hendrick, H. (ed.), *Child Welfare and Social Policy: An Essential Reader*. Bristol: Policy Press.
Macblain, S., Dunn, J., & Luke, I. 2017. *Contemporary Childhood*. London: Sage.
Macfarlane, K., & Lakhani, A. 2015. Performativity, Propriety and Productivity: The Unintended Consequences of Investing in the Early Years. *Contemporary Issues in Early Childhood*, 16, 179–191.
Miller, L., & Hevey, D. 2012. *Policy Issues in the Early Years*. Thousand Oaks, CA and London: Sage.
Morrissey, T. W., & Vinopal, K. 2018. Center-Based Early Care and Education and Children's School Readiness: Do Impacts Vary by Neighborhood Poverty? *Developmental Psychology*, 54, 757–771.
Moss, P., Dillon, J., & Statham, J. 2000. The 'Child in Need' and 'the Rich Child': Discourses, Constructions and Practice. *Critical Social Policy*, 20, 233–254.
Murray, J. 2017. Young Children are Human Beings. *International Journal of Early Years Education*, 25, 1–2.
Neaum, S. 2016. School Readiness and Pedagogies of Competence and Performance: Theorising the Troubled Relationship Between Early Years

and Early Years Policy. *International Journal of Early Years Education*, 24, 239–253.

NESS. 2012. *The Impact of Sure Start Local Programmes on Seven Year Olds and Their Families London: Institute for the Study of Children, Families and Social Issues*. Birkbeck: University of London.

Ofsted. 2017. Bold Beginnings: The Reception Curriculum in a Sample of Good and Outstanding Primary Schools. In: Ofsted (ed.). Manchester.

Palmer, S. 2009. What Is Toxic Childhood. In: House, R., & Loewenthal, D. (eds.), *Childhood, Well-Being, and a Therapeutic Ethos*. London: Karnac Books.

Rönkä, A., Malinen, K., Metsäpelto, R.-L., Laakso, M.-L., Sevón, E., & Verhoef-Van Dorp, M. 2017. Parental Working Time Patterns and Children's Socioemotional Wellbeing: Comparing Working Parents in Finland, the United Kingdom, and the Netherlands. *Children and Youth Services Review*, 76, 133–141.

Simpson, D., & Envy, R. 2015. Subsidizing Early Childhood Education and Care for Parents on Low Income: Moving Beyond the Individualized Economic Rationale of Neoliberalism. *Contemporary Issues in Early Childhood*, 16, 166–178.

Smith, F. 2013. Parents and Policy Under New Labour: A Case Study of the United Kingdom's New Deal for Lone Parents. *Children's Geographies*, 11, 160–172.

Smith, K. M. 2014. *The Government of Childhood: Discourse, Power and Subjectivity*. Basingstoke: Palgrave Macmillan.

Stirrup, J., Evans, J., & Davies, B. 2017a. Early Years Learning, Play Pedagogy and Social Class. *British Journal of Sociology of Education*, 38, 872–886.

Stirrup, J., Evans, J., & Davies, B. 2017b. Learning One's Place and Position Through Play: Social Class and Educational Opportunity in Early Years Education. *International Journal of Early Years Education*, 25, 343–360.

TACTYC. 2017. *Bald Beginnings* (Online). Association for Professional Development in Early Years. Available http://tactyc.org.uk/wp-content/uploads/2017/12/Bold-Beginnings-TACTYC-response-FINAL-09.12.17.pdf. Accessed 22 January 2018.

Tovey, H. 2007. *Playing Outdoors: Spaces and Places, Risk and Challenge*. Maidenhead: McGraw-Hill and Open University Press.

Turnbull, G. 2016. The Price of Youth: Commodification of Young People Through Malleable Risk Practices. *Journal of Youth Studies*, 19, 1007–1021.

Turnbull, G., & Spence, J. 2011. What's at Risk? The Proliferation of Risk Across Child and Youth Policy in England. *Journal of Youth Studies*, 14, 939–959.

Underdown, A., & Barlow, J. 2012. Promoting Infant Mental Health: A Public Health Priority and Approach. In: Miller, L. & Hevey, D. (eds.), *Policy Issues in the Early Years*. London: Sage.

Vincent, C. D., & Neis, B. L. 2011. Work and Family Life: Parental Work Schedules and Child Academic Achievement. *Community, Work & Family*, 14, 449–468.

Wells, K. 2018. *Childhood Studies*. Cambridge: Polity Press.

West, A., & Noden, P. 2016. Public Funding of Early Years Education in England: An Historical Perspective. *Clare Market Papers*, 21.

Wheway, R. 2008. *Not a Risk Averse Society: Fair Play for Children*. 2nd ed. Bognor Regis: Fair Play for Children.

Wilkes, S. 2011. *The Children History Forgot*. London: Robert Hale.

Williams, F. 2004. *Rethinking Families*. London: Calouste Gulbenkian Foundation.

Wyness, M. G. 2012. *Childhood and Society*. Basingstoke: Palgrave Macmillan.

6

Tameness at School

Abstract School is a major site for reinforcing a view of children as becomings and for the taming of childhood. Although schools promote the idea of developing individual character, many of their policies act to restrict it, and view children as objects to be processed. Children are expected to dress in a **uniform** manner and behave in a uniform manner. School **spaces**, such as **playgrounds**, are controlled to varying degrees in ways which restrict what children can do, sometimes for ostensibly safety reasons, and sometimes for the purposes of managing the school. **Testing** and **accountability** contribute to the ways in which children are subject to **datafication**, within a system whereby children are valued for what they contribute to the school.

Keywords Uniform · Spaces · Playgrounds · Testing · Accountability · Datafication

6.1 Introduction

By this point in the book, it should be clear that in terms of ideas about how children develop, there is a dominant discourse which tends to be defined by policy-makers which relates to the idea that children need to develop appropriately; this concern can be seen to reflect the debate as to whether or not children are becomings or beings with the dominant discourse clearly sitting within the becomings position. It is a position which has come to view what is deemed to be appropriate as that which will provide the desired outcomes. This can be seen in policy approaches such as Every Child Matters and Bold Beginnings, and is present in discussions about achieving potential. In recent years, it seems that the idea of potential has become ubiquitous in discussions and commentaries about education. It is a term that is quite seductive, but reveals a somewhat positivist understanding of children wherein potential is both unambiguous and finite (Creasy 2018). It is also a term which may reignite questions which rest upon social categories such as Class, Gender, or Ethnicity, especially in relation to what is appropriate with respect to education.

At the same time, although concerns about achieving potential may appear to reflect a concern for each individual child, it can be seen that in practice, it tends to reflect neoliberal concerns, in that they are situated within an economic context. Other aspects of potential, such as the potential to achieve emotional well-being, to develop spirituality or civic pride, are often ignored or negated. In most cases, potential is restricted to the potential to achieve certification with a view to employability and developments within education are increasingly adopting an approach wherein education is understood as a process within which uncertainty can be, and should be, reduced. Being confident in achieving a particular outcome by reducing uncertainty is a key characteristic of taming.

This chapter is about schools, but is not limited to education. Instead, the chapter considers the school as a location wherein taming takes place. As such, schools can be seen to adopt a number of practices which impact upon the lived experience of the child, and which restrict, or impoverish, what children can do. In this way, schools can be said to be a site for taming. It is important to note also that being educated and being schooled are not synonymous. We may go to school to be educated, but we are also schooled in ways which go beyond education.

There is also an argument, however, that education should provide the basis for agency (Divers 2017) as is encapsulated in the capabilities approach towards education (Buzzelli 2015). Schools in the UK often make much of the idea that they are concerned with children's individual self-development, but some practices adopted within schools provide evidence that undermines this argument. The endemic nature of school uniform polices, as discussed below, is but one example of the ways in which children are subject to forces which penalise individuality and which have the effect of taming children so as to create, in Foucault's words, docile bodies (Foucault 1979). The growth in denying children the right to talk to each other whilst at school, often referred to as a quiet corridors approach, is perhaps an extreme version of how schools act to tame childhood, reducing children to the level of objects to be processed (Booth 2018; Michaela 2018; Preece 2018; *Telegraph* 2018; Truelove 2018). Schools can be large organisations and we recognise the need to impose some form of structure in respect of how they operate. That said, we will argue that schools tend to privilege approaches which facilitate the processing of children rather than providing for the development of agency. In doing so, we will argue that the interests of the school have come to take precedence over the interests of each child.

6.2 School Spaces

The taming of childhood within school operates within a number of ways. For Pike and Kelly (2014), "schools are complex assemblages, governable spaces in which children and young people's bodies are regulated through a series of socio-spatial strategies and practices that seek to produce normative identities and govern children's bodies according to an existing array of social norms" (p. 101). One way in which this happens can be illustrated with respect to a very mundane, and somewhat hidden aspect of the school, the organisation of a school dining room (Pike and Kelly 2014; Pike 2008). This example shows how children are managed in a particular way and how this management divides children as a consequence of developing and applying rules relating to the eating of lunch (or dinner for some of us!).

Other aspects of the school estate which come to be managed in particular ways can also be considered. Pike and Kelly (2014) move beyond the dining room to analyse the way in which playgrounds can also be seen as a good example of how spaces that are ostensibly for children become managed in ways which tame the experience and which restrict their use in a number of ways. They illustrate how school reformers have previously seen playgrounds as areas within the school which provide scope for children to play freely, both mentally and physically. This freedom, however, is being lost.

It is over 40 years since we, the authors, left primary school and the climbing frame that stood proudly in the school playground that one of us attended is long gone. Standing around 3 m high on a tarmac base, this climbing frame always had children climbing and swinging on it during every break from school activities. A couple of adults were usually present in the playground and they did sometimes intervene with activities, but play was generally child led. As Thomson (2003) demonstrates though, the beginnings of playground interventions that were present by the end of the 1960s have become firmly entrenched in the contemporary playground. School staff are now very likely to impose a much more restricted experience than was once the case. As such, the experiences of children during playtime are strongly influenced by adult, and external, factors (Thomson 2003; Blatchford 1989). This has the consequence of restricting what activities may be engaged in, in spite of children's desires, in a way which results in a somewhat sterile, managed, and ultimately impoverished playtime. It seems that in spite of recent developments which seek to make the child's voice heard, it may not always be all that loud.

Concerns regarding health and safety are often presented as being to blame for the restriction of games such as tag, British Bulldog, and conkers, and the removal of equipment such as climbing frames (Hackett 2015; Schouten 2015; Wheway 2008; Gill 2007), but there is rarely any real compulsion behind this. This has led to what Hyndman and Telford (2015) refer to as 'surplus safety'. This reflects concerns first raised in Chapter 5 and with respect to this, Wheway (2008) illustrates how, in considerations of health and safety, it is invariably safety which takes precedence. However, the actions that are taken now, and which reduce or restrict, children's physical activities, ostensibly on the grounds of safety are likely to have longer term consequences for children's health. In restricting what children can do now though, we do not only impact upon children's possible future health, we also restrict their opportunities for growth and development by removing risk. As has been argued previously, risk is beneficial to growth and development. Children need challenges and risk is often an essential part of challenge (Harper 2017; Biesta 2013).

Health and safety is not the only concern though with respect to what happens within schools, Thomson (2003) illustrates how the concerns of school staff to maintain order also play a significant role in the taming of playtime. Alongside this, parental concerns regarding loss, damage, and injuries also exert influence over what is permitted at playtime. In a more extreme consequence for concerns about children's play though, even the opportunity for playtime is being restricted within some schools. The existence of bullying within the playground can be seen as one reason behind some schools reducing the time allocated to playtimes (Mulryan-Kyne 2014). In some schools, pupils are incorporated into the policing of playtime, though how children understand their role as playground monitors may be very different compared to how staff understand it (Sharma-Stray and Creasy 2013).

What becomes clear then is that within contemporary UK schools, playtime is rarely free time. Children are organised and restricted. They are subject to forms of surveillance but not only are they being observed, they are also often aware that they are being observed, (Richards 2012). They are also very aware of rules and regulations relating to playtimes (Thomson 2007).

6.3 Starting School, Meeting Targets, Becoming Data

It is no surprise that, globally, education, in the form of schooling, is very well established. This does not, however, imply that schooling has a universal position within all childhoods. Schooling is not the same for all children. The history of education within the UK demonstrates that approaches to schooling can and do change. For many children around the world, schooling starts at around the age of 7. In the UK, children are required to attend school much earlier (Murray 2017) and the nature of their school experience has become increasing formalised.

As was discussed in Chapter 5, the concept of schoolification can be seen to represent the tension between two different approaches to young children's learning and development. The Nordic social-pedagogic approach, with a focus on play, children's agency, and a sense of a developing self, can be contrasted with the formalised schooling approach that focuses upon an academic curriculum alongside achieving targets relating to learning (Broström 2017; Brogaard Clausen 2015; Dahlberg 2011). Broström points to the way in which global, political forces influence this debate by noting that with respect to the PISA league tables of educational achievement within different countries, the Nordic approach appears to be less successful. Young children experiencing the social-pedagogic approach do not perform as well as children experiencing a more formalised curriculum. However, this can be presented as demonstrating the benefits of formal schooling only where these benefits persist. As Broström demonstrates, the advantage does not persist throughout the child's life.

The issue of school readiness highlights the idea that childhood is a process that can, to an extent, be acted upon to achieve desired outcomes and that childhood itself may give rise to behaviours which are not welcome, especially in a school system which privileges formal approaches. These behaviours are often seen as the result of either parental failure or medical/health conditions so need to be identified and addressed through processes of early intervention. The contemporary focus on learning can be seen to contribute to concerns regarding what we mean by school readiness. In doing so, it may bring to the fore a concern with the way in which behaviours which are seen as childish are not conducive to learning. It always seems odd to us though that although much effort goes into establishing what it means to be a child through emphasising the "natural" characteristics of childhood, we then see social disdain for these characteristics.

In relation to this, Ofsted (2014) have drawn attention to what they see as constituting problematic behaviours within schools and classrooms which they categorise as low-level disruptions. Examples of what they mean by this are provided within this report and include 'Children talking between themselves when they should be listening; fiddling with anything; writing when they should be listening; refusing to work with a talk partner', and 'Chatting to neighbours; swinging on chairs; tapping pens; turning round; quietly humming; commenting quietly on something the teacher/a peer has said in class discussion; shouting out.' Both sets of examples are attributed to primary school teachers and are contained in a report referring to children aged from 5 (Ofsted 2014). If the early years are accepted as 0–5 as per the Early Years Foundation Stage, then we might consider that there is an expectation that children will be expected, required even, to not display such behaviours by this age. We do not see this as a realistic aim. This returns us to the question of what we mean by school readiness, as this may not be something that is shared by all. It may be better to consider that what is really meant by school readiness is readiness for a certain type of schooling.

So, although, ostensibly, the driving force behind early years and educational policy may be put forward as working in the best interests of the child, it can be seen that there are political concerns at work. For example, what can be referred to as the schoolification approach can be seen as a dominant discourse within the UK (Brogaard Clausen 2015). This reflects other aspects of early years policy in particular which has an impact upon schools such as the move towards baseline assessment of a child's performance. This then can also be seen as a further way in which to increase pressure upon schools with respect to accountability (Brogaard Clausen et al. 2015).

Accountability can be seen as fitting easily within the perspective which sees education as a process and which seeks identifiable and measurable outcomes. Such an approach has become well established within the UK Education system (Macfarlane 2017; Ball 2016; Hardy 2015; Roberts-Holmes 2015; Hargreaves 2003) as well as in other countries (Dorn and Ydesen 2014). In one sense, accountability dovetails with the range of testing methods adopted within the UK, in that a political concern to hold educators, not just teachers, accountable requires some mechanism for providing evidence. Testing plays that role. So, we may consider that the ongoing pressures which are brought to bear on children are driven, to a significant extent, by a concern that holds educators to account, rather than for pedagogic reasons. What this also gives rise to, and what will be considered next, is the way in which testing and assessment also contribute towards a changed way of understanding children. In particular, the way in which children become converted into data points through their relationship to the education system.

6.4 Metrics and the Datafication of Children

We have already argued that children are generally seen in terms of their future. This is intrinsic to the dominant view of children as becomings. We recognise that within academic circles, this may not be the case, that there may be more sophisticated ways of conceptualising childhood (Archard 2015), but suggest that amongst parents and practitioners, it is difficult to avoid this view. One of the ways in which this is manifest can be seen within the UK education system wherein ideas about the outcomes of education tend to dominate what happens within schools. This can be seen in debates about potential and added value. In a process-driven model of education, the intrinsic value of education in terms of self-development is negated in favour of a focus upon achievement. We can consider this as a shift from a concern with what children get out of school towards a concern with what they achieve at school with what counts as achievement limited to test scores or assessment outcomes.

One aspect of the ways in which childhood comes to be tamed may be seen as the way in which children, and by default, what they do, come to be transformed into data (Stevenson 2017; Roberts-Holmes and Bradbury 2016; Roberts-Holmes 2015). This data is then used to account for the actions of the school. In some ways, this provides for a further, unwelcome(?), development of taming, in that it suggests a denial of children as beings per se. Beer (2016) provides an underpinning account of this in respect to how concerns with surveillance have developed into the widespread use of metrics. For Beer, metrics are important in respect of the ways in which they intensify the control of populations. Datafication can be seen as the necessary precursor to the use of metrics and the school is a key location with respect to how children come to be understood, and understand themselves, as forms of data.

To be fair, it would be wrong to suggest that this process only operates within the school; children come to be transformed into data points even before birth (Lupton and Williamson 2017); it is very common to ask a question in relation to new-born children that reflects data, how much does the baby weigh, something that is then monitored over the next few years. However, as has been suggested above, the place of school within children's lives is such that this is an institution which has a significant ability to recast children in terms of data. This is not only with respect to how children are portrayed to others though, such as in terms of achievements via educational assessment. This also presents the data to children themselves. Children are often made very aware of the way in which they are viewed as data. This also reintroduces the idea that children may have agency, in that it provides for a consideration of how they may act to change that data.

In the early twenty-first century, it is difficult to ignore the role that data has come to play in our lives (Beer 2016; Lupton 2016). In many ways, the rise of smart phones and the plethora of apps that have been developed to cater for a myriad of concerns and interests have done much to position data as being central to our lives. This has both facilitated, and is driven by, a move towards a growing culture of self-tracking (Lupton 2016). The consequence of this is that it contributes towards a very particular way of understanding our sense of self. In some ways, this sense of understanding ourselves in relation to data is not particularly new for children. It is very common for children to see and represent themselves in terms of types of data. This has traditionally been in terms of age and height, but the growth in educational testing within the UK since the introduction of SATs in the late 1980s means that children are perhaps more attuned to a sense of educational position that they had been previously. We can also see the practice of "banding" within schools, or the introduction of identifying some children as "gifted and talented" as also contributing to a sense of position.

As Lupton (2016) illustrates though, the development of accessible and relatively cheap monitoring devices means that alongside educational achievements, children are increasingly being required to participate in the monitoring of their performance, such as in the case of physical education. This takes place within a cultural shift in which the generation of increased amounts of data is promoted as providing ways of improving service provision. This can be seen in the ways that developments in connectivity and monitoring are leading to the development of reporting platforms that are being marketed at schools, colleges, and universities under the guise of learning analytics (Clow 2013). In many ways, the rise of learning analytics represents one of the ways in which there is a demand for simple (tame) ways of understanding complex processes. As Wilson et al. (2017) note though, one thing that is often absent from claims about learning analytics is an unambiguous theory of what learning is. Learning analytics may tell us a lot about what pupils and students are doing, or where they are, but this is very often at a superficial level, they do not measure learning itself. They do, however, generate data and in doing so, contribute to datafication and the growing power of metrics.

We would suggest that there are problems with datafication. One problem relates to the way in which it often resists any sense of context. A second problem though is with regard to how any context that is admitted may come to be viewed as predictive. So, if it is the child's achievements which come to be reduced to data, it is seems fair to consider what this means for those children who are hampered in some way, in their attempts to become recorded as that data that is desirable. In a social context wherein each child's achievements become cast as a marker of the quality of a school, for example, through its position with league tables made up of each child's performance, it is possible to start to understand how children come to be ordered and where some children come to be seen positively, as in the Gifted and Talented scheme as introduced to UK schools. This was aimed at providing an academic challenge to pupils who were seen as being the most able (Koshy et al. 2012; Stewart 2006) within a general context of teachers being said to having low expectations (Radnor et al. 2007). The term Gifted and Talented is now discouraged, however, in favour of the most able. Where some children have been designated as Gifted and Talented, however, it can also be seen how some children come to be cast as undesirable. As such, it is appropriate to ask what datafication means for the child with SEND or the child whose home life is not conducive to educational success.

In some ways, the rise of datafication and its subsequent use within metrics such as learning analytics, can be seen as a further development of the evidence-based practice movement that has come to have significant influence within public services. The move towards evidence-based practice illustrates how ideas about what can be known about something can change, but also that this change may be contested, as some methods of knowing are seen as better or more useful than others (2001). Learning analytics can be seen as bound up with a scientific view of education. We are not intending to offer some anti-scientific argument here, but in following Rittel and Webber, we are cautious about applying a scientific lens to something which does not fit with the logic of science. For Rittel and Webber, scientific approaches can be seen as working very well with what they refer to as tame problems. They are not appropriate, however, when they are applied to situations that have their basis in social issues. This is because social issues, as was argued in Chapter 3, involve a level of complexity which resists a tame solution.

In considering why there is a growth in datafication then, we suggest that it is important to consider the political context. Political discourse may be seen to favour particular approaches, especially where they appear to provide a degree of certainty. As such, it is possible to see how datafication is easily accommodated, welcomed even, within a neoliberal perspective. This is because neoliberalism, in seeking to establish everything within a market model, tends to individualise and quantify. As part of the individualisation process, the social context is negated.

However, one of the main problems with seeing children's education as simply something to be processed is the myriad social influences which act upon them. This may be seen as contributing towards a need to tame childhood, to make children into something that can be processed by stripping away anything that might influence their experience and engagement with education, but it is something which is not really possible. For example, schools themselves are social and cultural organisations. They act in certain ways which impact upon children, some of which can clearly be seen as having the consequence of taming childhood.

6.5 Making School Uniform

As was argued earlier, although this chapter addresses the issue of schools, it is not wholly concerned with education. There are other aspects of schools which impact upon the taming of childhood. Reading through school prospectuses reveals a quite consistent theme of schools which aim to respect children as individuals and which seek to nurture and support that individuality. This is commendable. In practice however, schools often adopt policies and practices which appear to do the opposite of what they suggest that they aim for. This can be seen very clearly with respect to school uniform. Within the UK in particular, school uniform has significant importance and is often seen as an indicator or marker of standards as well as being promoted as an antidote to bullying and a means by which socio-economic differences can be obscured. This is not restricted to the UK; the global nature of these claims is illustrated by Deane (2015), commenting upon arguments for school uniforms within the US, not a country renowned for its adoption of school uniforms. Deane makes an important point though when she notes that "School uniform policies are not merely concerned with what one wears, but are a part of how we organize schools and the students therein" (2015: 113).

Indeed, Baumann and Krskova (2016) report that in countries where school uniforms are worn, there are identifiable benefits with regard to how pupils listen, the level of classroom noise, and in terms of lower waiting times within classes. This can be summarised as being as a consequence of uniforms leading to better school discipline when compared to where they are not adopted. As Brunsma and Rockquemore (2003) demonstrate, however, this does not necessarily translate into improved achievement. What researchers such as Brunsma and Rockquemore (2003) and Cribbie (2017) demonstrate is the difficulty of establishing positive outcomes, especially in terms of educational achievements, solely to the use of school uniforms. However, the extent to which this is the driving force behind the adoption of uniforms is questionable. Stephenson (2016) asserts that school uniform can be dated to the sixteenth-century charity schools and that poverty played a significant role in the adoption of a school uniform through the provision of clothing to those who needed it. However, although uniformity kept the costs of producing such clothing down, the adoption of particular colours also operated to signify both class and gender in a meaningful way, and, in doing so, to identify the social position of the wearer. The history of uniform use then is such as to suggest that educational achievement was always considered after the concern with the demonstration of social position, affiliation, or with respect to discipline. It has since become used to suggest or denote standards.

Stephenson (2016) suggests that the banning of corporal punishment within schools has had an impact upon school uniform being used to assert discipline. With respect to discipline, we are drawing upon a Foucauldian reading of the school within which the place and movement of bodies come to be an object for control (Clapham 2015; Bánovcanová and Masaryková 2014; Pike 2008). Although concerned with different issues within the school, each of these studies demonstrates ways in which power operates to produce particular outcomes, illustrating how Foucault's (1979) concept of docile bodies is manifest within the social practices of organisations. School uniform is one technique that can be utilised by the school as a way of restricting both individual and group expression. It is a technique which contributes to the taming of childhood.

That school uniform policies demonstrate power relations within the school which may act against the interests of pupils can be seen each September in the UK when it seems that rarely a year goes by without reports in the national press of large-scale exclusions of pupils who are deemed to have breached the uniform policy (Jarram and Pittam 2017; Phillips 2017; Lavigueur 2014; Star 2009). The examples referenced above are typical and usually result in pupils being excluded from school or placed in some form of isolation if they remain at school. As such, this throws up a paradox, in that the physical discipline that is exerted on to pupils for their failure to conform restricts their access to an education, something which the school is charged with providing. In this way, it is possible to argue that the school is valuing the docile child, for docile read tamed, more than it values the child as pupil; that is the child that is at school to learn.

What these exclusions often reveal, however, are the ways in which school policies privilege particular values or ideas. For example, in the case of Yewlands school in Sheffield (Star 2009), the Head teacher is quoted as stating "We have a new school building here, our results are up and we want our students to look professional and ready for the world of work" (n.p.). This is provided as a valid reason for not permitting pupils to wear trousers which she sees as inappropriate. She refers to "jeans-type" trousers which are designated as such as a consequence of the rear pockets being external, rather than internal. In making this statement though, the head is clearly privileging some types of work over others. It is not hard to consider that in expressing these views, the Head teacher is reinforcing a somewhat dated view relating to hierarchy and work. For those children whose parents do not wear what the Head teacher suggests is reflective of professional work, this can be understood as a social commentary of their value.

We are also reminded of a schoolteacher friend, teaching a class of 8-year olds, informing us of how she could spend 20 minutes each morning telling children that they are not in the correct uniform. This was reported in a manner that was deemed to be perfectly reasonable. Our concern here is that this may contribute to a degree of antagonism that is unhelpful. Teaching is always relational and scolding children who are reliant upon their parent's actions and emphasising that they are in the wrong does not seem to be conducive to developing positive relationships.

The issue of school uniform then is something that lends itself to problematising. We would argue that it occupies a dominant position within schools in the UK and can be seen to extend towards policies on hair. Schools seem to devote a significant amount of time and effort in restricting what pupils can wear, including the policing and sanctioning of those pupils whose hair is too long, too short, and even too patterned or the "wrong" colour. The reasons for this though are not because certain clothes, or certain hairstyles, prevent any child from learning. School uniform policies are always rooted within power relationships and reflect the aims of some to control others irrespective of the claims that are made in their defence.

In the example given above, the idea that the Head teacher is privileging some types of work above others reflects the argument that was raised earlier, that, for some, especially for neoliberals, school exists as a means by which to prepare children for work. This is a well-established principle. In some ways, the history of this position demonstrates that neoliberalism did not bring about this perspective, even though it is something that fits easily with neoliberal ideas. In some ways then, the Head teacher who rejects the wearing of a certain type of trouser because she holds a somewhat rigid, and possibly unrealistic view of what it means to look professional or which she claims does not demonstrate work-readiness, is presenting a contemporary version of correspondence theory (Bowles and Gintis 2011; Cole 1988). The basic argument presented by Bowles and Gintis is that the experiences, and hierarchy, of schools represent the sort of hierarchy that pupils will experience when entering the world of work. As a consequence, pupils learn particular behaviours and come to be versed in types of experiences that will be experienced during work whether that be giving orders or coping with the monotony and apparently pointless tasks that they will experience at school.

In this process of learning for later life, or at least in terms of learning to fit with a type of position reflecting later life, we see the idea of taming that is inherent within this. So, with respect to school uniform, pupils receive two discrete messages. One relates to the need to conform, and follow rules, irrespective of the banality of such rules.

The other message is that even in the post-industrial landscape of contemporary Western societies, some types of job are still ascribed with greater prestige. Children may be constantly informed that they can achieve anything, be anything even, but some achievements are clearly valued far more than others.

6.6 Conclusion: The Purpose of School

School is probably the most significant factor in respect of how society seeks to provide for development and opens questions regarding why society might see a need for education, what we mean by education, and what an educated child looks like. For Postman (1994), it was the development of printing that created the need for schools. Printing paved the way for a literate society and school became the means by which children enter this literate society. This opens a consideration of the distinction between education and training. We can see how there has always been a need for training with respect to crafts and techniques for production, even before industrialisation, but education is not the same as training. Training is focused upon acquiring the skills and abilities to reflect any particular task. Education is much broader.

At the same time, schools reflect a particular way of organising education which inevitably represents a departure from individualised approaches. This suggests that there is an extrinsic value to education as well as an intrinsic value. The view of education having an extrinsic value reflects the way in which education is seen in relation to society's needs, especially with respect to the economy. It is a utilitarian understanding of education. By this, we mean that education has some utility or use value. This can also be seen to reflect a neoliberal perspective of education in terms of how the economy requires particular skills and how the possession of such skills brings greater rewards in line with human capital theory (Hartog and Oosterbeek 2007). The idea of education as having an intrinsic value is found within a humanist tradition and is concerned with personal development.

The ubiquity of education around the globe lends itself to supporting the idea that there should be a right to education (Wrigley 2009), but having a right to it does not establish the nature of it. What the value or purposes of education is, or should be, is debatable (Pring 2004). Education is clearly important within society, but as Biesta (2009) notes, it has more than one function. Biesta points to three: qualification, socialisation, and subjectification. Within the argument that childhood is being tamed, we may consider that it is subjectification that has the greatest relevance with respect to taming, but all have some influence. In this way, we can see how schools contribute to a changing way of understanding children and childhood. In recent years, there seems to be an increased emphasis upon what children leave school with.

With respect to this, it seems to be the case that a significant factor in respect of how children come to be viewed is not in terms of themselves, as individuals, in spite of what schools may say. Instead, it is in terms of what children can achieve with respect to certification. It is certification that can be seen as the output that is achieved as a consequence of the process of education. This represents a departure, to some extent though, from the utilitarian perspective of education as introduced above. It was established above that the utilitarian position sees education as having utility, or use value, with respect to how it enables individuals to gain advantages within the economy, particularly with respect to the labour market. We do not reject this outright, but would point to the ways in which children's experiences of school have come to be viewed almost entirely in terms of what the child leaves the school with, which can be seen as certification. In this approach, certification comes to be seen as a proxy measure of education.

There is also a contradictory approach that can be taken with respect to education within the UK which departs from considering what the school provides to the child and, instead, considers what the child can bring to the school. In this scenario, the child that is more likely to succeed in achieving certification is likely to be valued more. As a consequence, we now appear to have a situation where the child has value, or not, based upon what they can provide to the school.

One thing which influences this is the way in which schools have come to be driven by targets. As schools come to see education as a process though, there is an increased pressure upon them to treat children as a means of achieving targets rather than as individuals in themselves.

This is to the extent that difficult or troublesome (untamed) children are increasingly excluded from schools. This can be seen in criticisms coming from Ofsted over schools that have come to reflect exam factories, a concern that could be traced back to the role that Ofsted has played in establishing such an approach (Ofsted and Spielman 2017) and which may be seen as driving moves to avoid this (Ofsted and Spielman 2018).

References

Archard, D. 2015. *Children: Rights and Childhood.* London: Routledge.
Ball, S. J. 2016. Neoliberal Education? Confronting the Slouching Beast. *Policy Futures in Education*, 14, 13.
Bánovcanová, Z., & Masaryková, D. 2014. The Docile Body—Reflecting the School. *Journal of Pedagogy*, 5, 251–264.
Baumann, C., & Krskova, H. 2016. School Discipline, School Uniforms and Academic Performance. *International Journal of Educational Management*, 30, 1003–1029.
Beer, D. 2016. *Metric Power.* New York: Palgrave Macmillan.
Biesta, G. J. J. 2009. Good Education in an Age of Measurement: On the Need to Reconnect with the Question of Purpose in Education. *Educational Assessment, Evaluation & Accountability*, 21, 33–46.
Biesta, G. J. J. 2013. *The Beautiful Risk of Education.* Boulder, CO: Paradigm Publishers.
Blatchford, P. 1989. *Playtime in the Primary School: Problems and Improvements.* Windsor: NFER-Nelson.
Booth, S. 2018. School Chat Ban for Kids in Corridors at Archway Academy. *Camden New Journal.*
Bowles, S., & Gintis, H. 2011. *Schooling in Capitalist America: Educational Reform and the Contradictions of Economic Life.* Chicago, IL: Haymarket.
Brew, A. 2001. *The Nature of Research: Inquiry in Academic Contexts.* London: Routledge.
Brogaard Clausen, S. 2015. Schoolification or Early Years Democracy? A Cross-Curricular Perspective from Denmark and England. *Contemporary Issues in Early Childhood*, 16, 355–373.
Brogaard Clausen, S., Guimaraes, S., Howe, S., & Cottle, M. 2015. Assessment of Young Children on Entry to School: Informative, Formative

or Performative? *International Journal for Cross-Disciplinary Subjects in Education*, 6, 5.

Broström, S. 2017. A Dynamic Learning Concept in Early Years' Education: A Possible Way to Prevent Schoolification. *International Journal of Early Years Education*, 25, 3–15.

Brunsma, D. L., & Rockquemore, K. A. 2003. Statistics, Sound Bites, and School Uniforms: A Reply to Bodine. *The Journal of Educational Research*, 97, 72–77.

Buzzelli, C. A. 2015. The Capabilities Approach: Rethinking Agency, Freedom, and Capital in Early Education. *Contemporary Issues in Early Childhood*, 16, 203–213.

Clapham, A. 2015. Producing the Docile Body: Analysing Local Area Under-Performance Inspection (LAUI). *Cambridge Journal of Education*, 45, 265–280.

Clow, D. 2013. An Overview of Learning Analytics. *Teaching in Higher Education*, 18, 683–695.

Cole, M. 1988. *Bowles and Gintis Revisited: Correspondence and Contradiction in Educational Theory*. London: Falmer Press.

Creasy, R. 2018. *The Taming of Education*. Basingstoke: Palgrave Macmillan.

Cribbie, R. A. 2017. Multiplicity Control, School Uniforms, and Other Perplexing Debates. *Canadian Journal of Behavioural Science / Revue canadienne des sciences du comportement*, 49, 159.

Dahlberg, G. 2011. Policies in Early Childhood Education and Care: Potentialities for Agency, Play and Learning. In: Corsaro, W. A., Qvortrup, J., & Honig, M.-S. (eds.), *The Palgrave Handbook of Childhood Studies*. Basingstoke: Palgrave Macmillan.

Deane, S. 2015. Dressing Diversity: Politics of Difference and the Case of School Uniforms. *Philosophical Studies in Education*, 46, 111–120.

Divers, A. 2017. Inculcating Agency. *Childhood & Philosophy*, 13, 253–270.

Dorn, S., & Ydesen, C. 2014. Towards a Comparative and International History of School Testing and Accountability. *Education Policy Analysis Archives*, 22, 1–11.

Foucault, M. 1979. *Discipline and Punish: The Birth of the Prison*. Harmondsworth: Penguin.

Gill, T. 2007. *No Fear: Growing Up in a Risk Averse Society*. London: Calouste Gulbenkian Foundation.

Hackett, J. 2015. Top 10 Worst Health and Safety Myths. *Manager: British Journal of Administrative Management*, 2nd Quarter, 22–23, 2p.

Hardy, I. 2015. A Logic of Enumeration: The Nature and Effects of National Literacy and Numeracy Testing in Australia. *Journal of Education Policy*, 30, 335–362.

Hargreaves, A. 2003. *Teaching in the Knowledge Society: Education in the Age of Insecurity*. New York: Teachers College Press.

Harper, N. J. 2017. Outdoor Risky Play and Healthy Child Development in the Shadow of the "Risk Society": A Forest and Nature School Perspective. *Child & Youth Services*, 38, 318–334.

Hartog, J., & Oosterbeek, H. 2007. What Should You Know About the Private Returns to Education? In: Hartog, J., & Maassen Van Den Brink, H. (eds.), *Human Capital: Advances in Theory and Evidence*. Cambridge: Cambridge University Press.

Hyndman, B. P., & Telford, A. 2015. Should Educators Be "Wrapping School Playgrounds in Cotton Wool" to Encourage Physical Activity? Exploring Primary and Secondary Students' Voices from the School Playground. *Australian Journal of Teacher Education*, 40, 4.

Jarram, M., & Pittam, D. 2017. *71 Students Put in Isolation for Wearing the Wrong Uniform on School's First Day of Term* (Online). Available http://www.nottinghampost.com/news/nottingham-news/71-students-put-isolation-wearing-437316. Accessed 12 January 2018.

Koshy, V., Pinheiro-Torres, C., & Portman-Smith, C. 2012. The Landscape of Gifted and Talented Education in England and Wales: How Are Teachers Implementing Policy? *Research Papers in Education*, 27, 167–186.

Lavigueur, N. 2014. *The Wrong Trousers: Parents Angry After Pupils Put in Isolation at Colne Valley High School on First Day Back for 'Incorrect Trousers'* (Online). Available http://www.examiner.co.uk/news/west-yorkshire-news/wrong-trousers-parents-angry-after-7708277. Accessed 12 January 2018.

Lupton, D. 2016. *The Quantified Self*. Cambridge: Polity Press.

Lupton, D., & Williamson, B. 2017. The Datafied Child: The Dataveillance of Children and Implications for Their Rights. *New Media & Society*, 19, 780–794.

Macfarlane, B. 2017. *Freedom to Learn: The Threat to Student Academic Freedom and Why It Needs to Be Reclaimed*. Abingdon: Routledge.

Michaela. 2018. *RE: Michaela Behaviour Policy*.

Mulryan-Kyne, C. 2014. The School Playground Experience: Opportunities and Challenges for Children and School Staff. *Educational Studies*, 40, 377–395.

Murray, J. 2017. Young Children are Human Beings. *International Journal of Early Years Education*, 25, 1–2.

Ofsted. 2014. *Below the Radar: Low-Level Disruption in the Country's Classrooms*. London: Ofsted.

Ofsted, & Spielman, A. 2017. *Amanda Spielman's Speech at the ASCL Annual Conference* (Online). HM Government. Available https://www.gov.uk/government/speeches/amanda-spielmans-speech-at-the-ascl-annual-conference. Accessed 24 March 2017.

Ofsted, & Spielman, A. 2018. *Amanda Spielman Speech to the Schools NorthEast Summit* (Online). London: Ofsted. Available https://www.gov.uk/government/speeches/amanda-spielman-speech-to-the-schools-northeast-summit. Accessed 18 October 2018.

Phillips, J. 2017. *Pupils Banned from Cheltenham Bournside School for Wearing Wrong Trousers* (Online). Available http://www.gloucestershirelive.co.uk/news/cheltenham-news/pupils-banned-cheltenham-bournside-school-432153. Accessed 12 January 2017.

Pike, J. 2008. Foucault, Space and Primary School Dining Rooms. *Children's Geographies*, 6, 413–422.

Pike, J., & Kelly, P. 2014. *The Moral Geographies of Children, Young People and Food: Beyond Jamie's School Dinners*. Basingstoke: Palgrave Macmillan.

Postman, N. 1994. *The Disappearance of Childhood*. New York: Vintage.

Preece, A. 2018. 'Prison-Like' School Tells Pupils to Walk Between Classes in Silence at Ninestiles, An Academy. *Birmingham Live*.

Pring, R. 2004. *Philosophy of Education: Aims, Theory, Common Sense and Research*. London: Continuum.

Radnor, H., Koshy, V., & Taylor, A. 2007. Gifts, Talents and Meritocracy. *Journal of Education Policy*, 22, 283–299.

Richards, C. 2012. Playing Under Surveillance: Gender, Performance and the Conduct of the Self in a Primary School Playground. *British Journal of Sociology of Education*, 33, 373–390.

Roberts-Holmes, G. 2015. The 'Datafication' of Early Years Pedagogy: 'If the Teaching Is Good, the Data Should Be Good and If There's Bad Teaching, There Is Bad Data'. *Journal of Education Policy*, 30, 302–315.

Roberts-Holmes, G., & Bradbury, A. 2016. Governance, Accountability and the Datafication of Early Years Education in England. *British Educational Research Journal*, 42, 600–613.

Schouten, L. 2015. Ban on 'Tag': Are School Children Getting the Right Playtime? *Christian Science Monitor*.

Sharma-Stray, L., & Creasy, R. 2013. Children as Playtime Monitors: What It Means for the Monitor. *Pastoral Care in Education*, 31, 229–239.

Star, T. 2009. *Children Sent Home from School for Wearing Wrong Trousers* (Online). Sheffield. Available https://www.thestar.co.uk/whats-on/out-and-about/children-sent-home-from-school-for-wearing-wrong-trousers-1-297085. Accessed 12 January 2018.

Stephenson, K. 2016. *"It's Not for the Sake of a Ribboned Coat": A History of British School Uniform*. University of York.

Stevenson, H. 2017. The "Datafication" of Teaching: Can Teachers Speak Back to the Numbers? *Peabody Journal of Education*, 92, 537–557. https://doi.org/10.1080/0161956X.2017.1349492.

Stewart, W. 2006. New Register for the Gifted and Talented. *TES: Times Educational Supplement*.

Telegraph. 2018. Pupils Banned from Talking While Walking Between Lessons Under Headteacher's Silence Policy. *Daily Telegraph*.

Thomson, S. 2003. A Well-Equipped Hamster Cage: The Rationalisation of Primary School Playtime. *Education 3–13*, 31, 54–59.

Thomson, S. 2007. Do's and Don'ts: Children's Experiences of the Primary School Playground. *Environmental Education Research*, 13, 487–500.

Truelove, S. 2018. Croydon School Bans Pupils from Talking in Corridors and Says It Has Transformed Behaviour. *Croydon Advertiser*.

Wheway, R. 2008. *Not a Risk Averse Society: Fair Play for Children*. 2nd ed. Bognor Regis: Fair Play for Children.

Wilson, A., Watson, C., Thompson, T. L., Drew, V., & Doyle, S. 2017. Learning Analytics: Challenges and Limitations. *Teaching in Higher Education*, 22, 991–1007.

Wrigley, T. 2009. Rethinking Education in the Era of Globalization. In: Hill, D. (ed.), *Contesting Neo-Liberal Education: Public Resistance and Collective Advance*. Abingdon: Routledge.

7

Conclusion

Abstract This chapter revisits the basic argument of the book that **childhood** is being subject to socio-political forces which are shaping it in ways which restrict and impoverish children's lived experiences. This contributes to a childhood that does not prepare children for their future, nor provide scope for their **development**. A tame childhood contributes to the mental and **emotional problems** which children increasingly report. In concluding, we point to the fallacy that things are done in the **best interests** of children and provide pointers to the manner in which a tame childhood can be resisted in ways which give scope to children to try and, sometimes, fail. Children need some **freedom**, but that does not mean that they have no **boundaries**.

Keywords Childhood · Development · Emotional problems · Best interests · Freedom · Boundaries

7.1 Introduction

As conclusions are wont to do, this chapter draws the arguments together and proposes that contemporary approaches towards childhood and parenting are taming the experience of childhood and, as a consequence, this is impoverishing children's lives. In saying this, we are putting forward an argument in which the cumulative effects of actions which impact upon children or which shape childhood operate as a form of violence against children. This is because actions which serve to tame childhood deny children the opportunities which are necessary for the development and maintenance of resilience, and we see resilience as necessary to enable both a fulfilled childhood and a functioning adulthood. Furthermore, this form of violence denies children their rights to agency. In this respect, it undermines their position as beings.

In part though, we consider that the taming to which we refer often rests upon a somewhat restricted view of childhood. This restricted view, as argued above, is predominantly shaped by our notions of how a child fits into our society and is strongly influenced by political ideology. This is one reason why children who fail to reflect the idealised version of childhood cause consternation, in both what they do and/or their social position. Because of this, children who do not fit the idealised view are likely to exacerbate policies and practices which have the effect of taming childhood. We see this being enacted in policy developments which operate as reactions to particular concerns. For example, children who engage in illegal or sexual activities can be seen as examples of those children who are in some way needing to be tamed. It can be seen that there are similar concerns regarding those parents deemed to be hard to reach, a term which conveniently locates the problem with the parents. In both cases, support tends to be mobilised by recourse to the ways in which not doing anything will have negative consequences for the future of society. This rests upon a view of children as becoming within the more general context of seeing children as the future in waiting with only one opportunity to get it right.

If children really are the future, then we argue that we need children to develop into adults who are resilient, creative, and able. Whilst this view may not be shared by everyone, it can be seen that a tame childhood is not an appropriate childhood from which to develop. We can see how policy-makers work with a view of what they want to achieve, but we have concerns that in seeing childhood in terms of a process within a one-off opportunity, there is an inclination to attempt to remove uncertainty so as to ensure that the aims that adults have for children are achieved. This uncertainty often translates into an attempt to remove any and all potential risks from children's lives. Our concern is that this may act against children's individuality and impede the scope for their development. We argue for a recognition that childhood requires freedom if we are to ensure that children are to develop into well-rounded adults. This freedom may be accompanied, however, by some degree of risk. However, if we want children to develop resilience and self-determination, we will not help them by restricting what they can do and attempting to remove all risk from their lives. In sum, a tame childhood is an impoverished childhood. Furthermore, attempts to remove risk from children's lives can result in unintended consequences for children that present, if not a greater threat, certainly an equal threat to children's well-being.

We have suggested throughout this book that there is no one factor which has led to childhood being tamed. Instead, we can see how changes in a number of factors intersect and lead to a childhood that for very many children within the UK differs markedly from that experienced by previous generations. Whilst the past should not be idealised, it is important to acknowledge that whilst material conditions for children may have improved generally, something has been lost in the restrictions placed on children in contemporary society. This seems to fly in the face of anxieties that arose with the growth of the rights of the child agenda which saw some concerned that children would hold greater rights than adults and thus would become uncontrollable. In one sense, Bronfenbrenner's (1979) socio-ecological model provides a useful starting point for considering how forces which operate at different levels can have a cumulative effect of taming childhood, especially when a chronological consideration is taken into account so as to accommodate the dynamic, and changing, nature of social life.

One significant change can be seen as the way in which the development and adoption of communications technologies has led to a generation which from before birth, has been recorded, documented, and shared. Importantly though, this does not take place in a passive manner, carried out by others. For very many children within the UK, the recording, documentation, and the sharing of this are carried out by themselves and their friends. This has led to a way of living that is public, open to comment and judgement and can be seen as less tolerant of difference or diversity in the broadest sense.

In turn, this creates a paradox, in that in a society in which it is known that children and young people are experiencing increasing problems with respect to mental health and where they are subject to significant stressors within their lives, there is a seemingly increasing pressure to appear happy and to be having a good time. This can be seen within what Storr (2017) calls 'selfie culture'. No one factor 'causes' selfie culture. Taken together though, selfie culture becomes manifest. A consideration of selfie culture illustrates the conflict between becoming and being as played out within the taming of childhood. As we have said previously, practitioners, parents, and policy-makers may see children in terms of becoming, but, for children, there is significant pressure in terms of their being.

So, following the argument above that our social context is shaped by ways in which different factors intersect, we can see that the individualism that is privileged by neoliberalism intersects with the development of technology that intensifies a concern with public identity and promotes a form of narcissism. These factors come together in a way that changes the understanding and engagement with respect to identity and communication. However, very often, it seems that rather than broadening possible identities for children, it often restricts them by promoting certain identities as being not only ideal but easily attainable. This leads to an experience where they see themselves as either being the ideal or not, but these ideals are so restrictive and prescriptive that children do not take risks to form their own identity.

7.2 What's Best for Children?

We want to start this section by repeating something that was brought up earlier; the oft-quoted mantra that all parents want what is best for their children. A version of this is even presented by Layard and Dunn (2009) in writing up the first of the Children's Society reports on modern childhood. Whilst this is evidently not true if we consider those children in our society who are harmed on a daily basis, it is also another example of something which tends to operate at a superficial level. Helicopter parents as considered in Chapter 4 may claim to want what is best for their children, but, as was demonstrated, the intensive parenting that some children receive is not at all in their long-term interests and could be argued to be more about the parents' own needs than the needs to the child. What was argued in Chapter 4 then is that at a family level, there have been developments with respect to parenting, which means that many children have restricted opportunities to engage with their environment and to develop their abilities and resilience. As such, although those parents who provide intensive parenting may appear to be trying to do the best for their children, and may assure themselves that they are a good parent, the long-term outcomes for children are unlikely to be positive (Perry et al. 2018). Furthermore, even where parents acknowledge the possible negative consequences for children, for example, confining children to the home leading to excess screen time in whatever format, they feel unable to find a solution to this.

However, what has also been considered throughout the book is the way in which parents are not solely responsible for the taming of childhood. It may well be the case that paranoid parents, or parents who are overly sensitive to social ideas about what it means to be a good parent play a significant part in taming, but they are responding to a society that holds them accountable if things go wrong for their child, with dire consequences being possible when this happens. As such, we have considered how schools and the government also play a major part. In some ways, schools pose a particularly frustrating example in that, although their primary purpose is to provide an education for children, there are many ways in which they act to tame childhood in an attempt to provide an education which has become increasingly restricted by the National Curriculum. Furthermore, such policies such as school uniforms, which have no significant evidence for being useful, were presented as a particular example of this and it is very hard to see how school uniforms can be justified on educational grounds.

Alongside the problems which schools cause for children and parents with respect to appearance, we have also demonstrated how the power of schools comes to bear on children for the purpose of establishing a particular representation of the school rather than a concern for each child. In large part though, this has been driven by government concerns and can be epitomised in the way that data has been elevated in terms of its social position. As children become data points, so they are denied a sense of self. It would be very difficult to argue that viewing children as data points is in the best interests of children; yet, in practice, this is what happens, feeding the notion that children have only one chance at achieving the necessary skills to progress whilst restricting the skills taught to a tame tick list.

For parents then, providing what is best for their children is not easy. In part, this is because we cannot really know what is best for children, but also, as we have shown, parents operate within a context whereby there are social pressures to parent in particular ways. Part of the pressure on parents comes from Governments and they too may claim that what they do is in the best interests of children. However, Governments may claim to want the best for the children within their society but then introduce policies which do not benefit children or result in unintended consequences. That is not to say that they do not intend to improve children's lives but that they may not have the foresight to understand the impact policies will have on children's lives, or the courage to offer radical solutions that may not be politically popular.

Education policies are a good example of what we mean by this. Some parts of the UK have retained a selective system of education which was established to cater for UK society as it was in the 1940s. This is intrinsic to the tripartite system, established by the 1944 Education Act as putting children on a track to become managers, craft workers, or unskilled workers. This is reflected in Grammar schools,

Technical schools, and Secondary Modern schools. The system as a whole allocates children to different schools based upon performance in a test at the age of 11. Most readers will recognise this as being what is referred to as the Grammar school system. There is a recurring theme in UK politics which calls for a return to this system across the country as a whole and in 2016, the Conservative Government reignited such debates by seeming to suggest that this system would be extended. Promoters of the Grammar school system generally argue that it provides opportunities for poorer children in particular to achieve better educational outcomes. Because of how the UK education system is set up, it is not easy to support this claim. It has, however, been argued that poorer children in general are not well served by this system (Andrews et al. 2016; Coe et al. 2008). In addition to this though, the economy of the UK in the twenty-first century is very different from the middle of the twentieth century and such specific employment options no longer exist. Furthermore, to determine an individual's future at age 11 appears nonsensical.

In general though, support for Grammar schools tends to rest on the idea that these are better types of schools. That may be true, but if we want what is best for children it can be questioned how setting up a system wherein some schools are better than others actually achieves its aims if it means that by definition some children will be required to attend schools that are not as good as others by design. This seems to be exacerbated if it becomes evident that the schools which are seen as being less good will be reserved for the children who do not do as well in educational terms at age 11 which is generally evidenced to be those children from lower socio-economic groups. To put this in context, it would be hard to imagine a policy proposal which established two levels of provision in any other aspect of public provision, wherein one level is better resourced and where one would be less well resourced. Education appears to be the only real area of public provision where it seems acceptable to claim that some individuals are in some way deserving of better levels of publicly provided service.

So, although the claim that society will naturally want what is best for children is something that is often and easily stated, there is little depth to it. Firstly, it is difficult to identify what is best for children;

what is the definition of a good childhood? Furthermore, we may want something, but it becomes very difficult to establish how this can be achieved when we would need to disentangle what we want from the range of policy, practice, and discourse which constitutes the context within which it exists. What we, the authors, would want is for childhood to not be tame.

7.3 Resisting Tameness

In one sense, we are ending with a consideration of what we would actually want for children. This returns us to an earlier reference to Tobin et al. (2011) who identify that childhood is shaped to fit a particular culture. In this sense, we provide for children with less of an idea as to how children live their daily lives but more with an idea of what we want children to become. We could boil this down to one very concise idea: we want our children to cope. This seems indisputable if we agree as a society that we want the best for children. In wanting our children to cope though, we would argue that this requires that children develop resilience and are able to reinforce, and even extend, their resilience throughout their lives.

Not all children are coping. And whilst, throughout time, a number of children would be in this position, this appears to becoming an increasing number. We established in Chapter 1 that increasing numbers of children and young people are experiencing mental health issues. We, in our role as academic staff in Higher Education, seem to have growing numbers of undergraduate students each year who profess that they feel a level of anxiety and stress that prohibits them from undertaking expected steps for development such as being able to present to a group of their peers. Taking these together, it seems that increasing numbers of children are not coping with what is simply everyday life. Our concern throughout this book has been to consider a range of ways that children are being restricted in respect of their lived experiences in ways which mean that they are not able to develop, maintain, and reinforce resilience. We have contextualised this as a general taming of childhood. In a nutshell, we have argued that the lived experiences of many children within the UK is one that is limited in many ways and that this undermines the way in which they develop as individuals and the way in which they are able to develop resilience.

In charting how what we do to, and for, children works against their best interests, we arrive at a problem, namely what shall we do for, and to, children that would be of benefit? With reference to Rittel and Webber (1973), this may well be expressed as a wicked problem. It will certainly not be a tame solution. Nor will it be something that is easy for there is likely to be resistance to embedding some of the responses to taming that we might consider as being necessary. That said, there is already some recognition of the problem, but whilst there may be some resistance to the problems, there will also be resistance to the solutions. As an accessible approach to avoiding the taming of childhood though we feel that the following points are pertinent:

1. Accept that accidents do happen. Children need to extend themselves and sometimes this will result in a grazed a knee or a cut finger. When children's physical activities are curtailed or when they are restricted in their activities because of concerns about safety, this can be seen as restricting their development. There is also a need to consider what this means for their long-term health (Wheway 2008). In a society that seems to be increasingly concerned about a sedentary lifestyle and obesity, it seems to be wrong to restrict children's physical activities;
2. Recognise that children can be resourceful and capable and act on that recognition. It is too easy to say that children are resourceful and then plan activities that do not allow them to flourish. The way in which the forest school model has been interpreted in this country very often does not go as far as the original Danish models would wish. As a consequence an entrenched, learned belief that children are vulnerable becomes manifest in what we provide for them. The opportunity to try something new or difficult, even if this sees them failing, is better than avoiding having a go at something new or challenging;

3. Accept that children are able to make their own decisions. They may not make the decision that adults would come to, but as novice decision-makers they need to be able to make some decisions as part of their development. Making all of a child's decisions for them, including what, and how, to play will not be helpful to them;
4. Recognise that children are quite capable of playing on their own, without adult direction and/or supervision. It is acceptable for children to experience boredom for this gives a child space to make decisions and be creative. It is also acceptable for a child to enjoy solitude;
5. None of this means that children should not have boundaries and, in relation to decision-making, this does not mean that they should be given into, rather that the reasons for over-riding their wishes should be explained. In a social sense, all individuals have boundaries. If we are to treat children as beings, rather than becomings, it is important that children are treated respectfully, in a way that supports their development. Boundaries contribute to this.

In concluding, it should be considered that by resisting tameness in childhood, we open up space for children's agency, something that the children's rights movement spearheaded by the UNCRC intended in its call for participation. Resisting tameness provides opportunities for them to develop as beings rather than move through predetermined milestones as becomings. We have said previously that in academic debates, the view of children as beings rather than becomings is well established. We have also said, however, that from the position of parents, practitioners, and governments this is less well accepted possibly because being a child appears fraught with all sorts of risks and challenges. We do not see parents, practitioners, or governments ascribing to a view which sees children as having any real validity within their own right and providing scope for children's agency as a consequence. It may well be though that should each of these start to see children as beings, then this would be a significant move towards resisting tameness within childhood.

Accepting children as beings inevitably creates pressures to accept their agency, to see them as having scope for self-determination.

This is not a call to permit all behaviours, but it is a call to give children greater scope. However, the evident anxiety that seems to arise from giving children agency, which, it is said, will lead to permissiveness and result in negative outcomes needs to be addressed. Just because children have choice or knowledge or even power, it does not mean that this will lead to negative outcomes for them. For example, not all children use illegal drugs despite the fact they are prevalent in our society. Not all children partake in underage sex even though they have ample opportunity to do this.

This is not a call for a childhood without rules or boundaries. We consider that children thrive best when they know what boundaries are in place and when they can be confident that such boundaries are stable. The importance of a sense of security with respect to children's development has a long history (Van Rosmalen et al. 2015, 2016) and it can be seen how security in this sense rests upon the level of stability demonstrated in parenting.

However, these boundaries can be negotiable and are more likely to be effective if children have some part in agreeing them and understanding why they are in place. It is not beneficial, however, for children to be faced with boundaries that are restricted or rigid. Boundaries should not only be movable, so as to accommodate the child's development, they need to have some degree of elasticity embedded within them. As children grow and develop, we should expect them to push on the boundaries that they are faced with. In this way, the child provides indicators to parents that they may be capable of more than was once the case. In such situations though, parents must acknowledge that sometimes children will push too fast or too far. As a consequence, children may find that sometimes, parents were right, that they were not quite ready, but a child's failings are not necessarily the same as a parents failing. For children, failing can be a learning experience. In a childhood that is tame, opportunities for learning, for growth and development, are restricted and if this is the childhood that we provide, we should not be surprised if our children demonstrate limitations as adults.

References

Andrews, J., Hutchinson, J., & Johnes, R. 2016. *Grammar Schools and Social Mobility*. London: Education Policy Institute.

Bronfenbrenner, U. 1979. *The Ecology of Human Development: Experiments by Nature and Design*. Cambridge, MA: Harvard University Press.

Coe, R., Jones, K., Searle, J., Kokotsaki, D., Mohd Kosnin, A., & Skinner, P. 2008. *Evidence on the Effects of Selective Educational Systems*. Durham: CEM Centre and Durham University.

Layard, R., & Dunn, J. 2009. *A Good Childhood: Searching for Values in a Competitive Age*. London: Penguin.

Perry, N. B., Dollar, J. M., Calkins, S. D., Keane, S. P., & Shanahan, L. 2018. Childhood Self-Regulation as a Mechanism Through Which Early Overcontrolling Parenting Is Associated with Adjustment in Preadolescence. *Developmental Psychology*, 54, 1542–1555.

Rittel, H. W. J., & Webber, M. M. 1973. Dilemmas in a General Theory of Planning. *Policy Sciences*, 4, 155–169.

Storr, W. 2017. *Selfie: How We Became So Self-Obsessed and What It's Doing to Us*. London: Picador.

Tobin, J., Hsueh, Y., & Karasawa, M. 2011. *Preschool in Three Cultures Revisited: China, Japan, and the United States*. Chicago, IL: University of Chicago Press.

Van Rosmalen, L., Van der Horst, F. C. P., & Van der Veer, R. 2016. From Secure Dependency to Attachment: Mary Ainsworth's Integration of Blatz's Security Theory into Bowlby's Attachment Theory. *History of Psychology*, 19, 22.

Van Rosmalen, L., Van der Veer, R., & Van der Horst, F. 2015. Ainsworth's Strange Situation Procedure: The Origin of an Instrument. *Journal of the History of the Behavioral Sciences*, 51, 261–284.

Wheway, R. 2008. *Not a Risk Averse Society: Fair Play for Children*. 2nd ed. Bognor Regis: Fair Play for Children.

References

Action for Children. 2018. *Mental Health for Young People* (Online). Watford. Available https://www.actionforchildren.org.uk/what-we-do/our-impact/mental-health-overview/mental-health-for-young-people/. Accessed 18 October 2018.

Amable, B. 2011. Morals and Politics in the Ideology of Neo-Liberalism. *Socio-Economic Review*, 9, 3–30.

Anderson, D. L., & Graham, A. P. 2016. Improving Student Wellbeing: Having a Say at School. *School Effectiveness & School Improvement*, 27, 348–366.

Andrews, J., Hutchinson, J., & Johnes, R. 2016. *Grammar Schools and Social Mobility*. London: Education Policy Institute.

Anning, A., & Ball, M. 2008. *Improving Services for Young Children: From Sure Start to Children's Centres*. Los Angeles, CA and London: Sage.

Archard, D. 2015. *Children: Rights and Childhood*. London: Routledge.

Aries, P. 1962. *Centuries of Childhood: A Social History of Family Life*. New York, NY: Vintage Books.

Aynsley-Green, A. 2018. *The British Betrayal of Childhood*. London: Routledge.

Ball, S. J. 2016. Neoliberal Education? Confronting the Slouching Beast. *Policy Futures in Education*, 14, 13.

Bánovcanová, Z., & Masaryková, D. 2014. The Docile Body—Reflecting the School. *Journal of Pedagogy*, 5, 251–264.

References

Baraldi, C., & Cockburn, T. 2018. Introduction: Lived Citizenship, Rights and Participation in Contemporary Europe. In: Baraldi, C., & Cockburn, T. (eds.), *Theorising Childhood: Citizenship, Rights and Participation*. Cham: Springer.

Barbalet, J. M. 1998. *Emotion, Social Theory & Social Structure: Towards a Macrosociological Approach*. Cambridge: Cambridge University Press.

Barnes, J., Belsky, J., & Melhuish, E. C. 2007. *The National Evaluation of Sure Start: Does Area-Based Early Intervention Work?* Bristol: Policy Press.

Baumann, C., & Krskova, H. 2016. School Discipline, School Uniforms and Academic Performance. *International Journal of Educational Management*, 30, 1003–1029.

Beck, U. 1992. *Risk Society: Towards a New Modernity*. London: Sage.

Beer, D. 2016. *Metric Power*. New York: Palgrave Macmillan.

Ben-Arieh, A. 2006. Is the Study of the "State of Our Children" Changing? Re-visiting After 5 Years. *Children and Youth Services Review*, 28, 799–811.

Biesta, G. J. J. 2009. Good Education in an Age of Measurement: On the Need to Reconnect with the Question of Purpose in Education. *Educational Assessment, Evaluation & Accountability*, 21, 33–46.

Biesta, G. J. J. 2013. *The Beautiful Risk of Education*. Boulder, CO: Paradigm Publishers.

Blackman, T., Elliott, E., Greene, A., Harrington, B., Hunter, D. J., Marks, L., Mckee, L., & Willimas, G. 2006. Performance Assessment and Wicked Problems: The Case of Health Inequalities. *Public Policy and Administration*, 21, 66–80.

Blatchford, P. 1989. *Playtime in the Primary School: Problems and Improvements*. Windsor: NFER-Nelson.

Bond, E. 2010. Managing Mobile Relationships: Children's Perceptions of the Impact of the Mobile Phone on Relationships in Their Everyday Lives. In: *Childhood-Copenhagen Then London-Munksgaard Then Sage*, 17, 514–529.

Bond, E. 2013. Mobile Phones, Risk and Responsibility: Understanding Children's Perceptions. *Cyberpsychology*, 7, Article 3.

Booth, S. 2018. School Chat Ban for Kids in Corridors at Archway Academy. *Camden New Journal*.

Bore, A., & Wright, N. 2009. The Wicked and Complex in Education: Developing a Transdisciplinary Perspective for Policy Formulation, Implementation and Professional Practice. *Journal of Education for Teaching*, 35, 241–256.

Bottery, M. 2016. *Educational Leadership for a More Sustainable World*. London: Bloomsbury.

Bowles, S., & Gintis, H. 2011. *Schooling in Capitalist America: Educational Reform and the Contradictions of Economic Life*. Chicago, IL: Haymarket.

BPAS. 2018. *Social Media, SRE, and Sensible Drinking: Understanding the Dramatic Decline in Teenage Pregnancy*. Stratford: British Pregnancy Advisory Service.

Bradshaw, J. (ed.). 2016. *The Well-Being of Children in the UK*. Bristol: Policy Press.

Bradshaw, J., Hoelscher, P., & Richardson, D. 2007. An Index of Child Well-Being in the European Union. *Social Indicators Research*, 80, 133–177.

Brew, A. 2001. *The Nature of Research: Inquiry in Academic Contexts*. London: Routledge.

Bridges, D. 2010. Government's Construction of the Relation Between Parents and Schools in the Upbringing of Children in England: 1963–2009. *Educational Theory*, 60, 299–324.

Bristow, J. 2014. The Double Bind of Parenting Culture: Helicopter Parents and Cotton Wool Kids. In: Lee, E., Bristow, J., Faircloth, C., & Macvarish, J. (eds.), *Parenting Culture Studies*. New York, NY: Palgrave Macmillan.

Brogaard Clausen, S. 2015. Schoolification or Early Years Democracy? A Cross-Curricular Perspective from Denmark and England. *Contemporary Issues in Early Childhood*, 16, 355–373.

Brogaard Clausen, S., Guimaraes, S., Howe, S., & Cottle, M. 2015. Assessment of Young Children on Entry to School: Informative, Formative or Performative? *International Journal for Cross-Disciplinary Subjects in Education*, 6, 5.

Bronfenbrenner, U. 1979. *The Ecology of Human Development: Experiments by Nature and Design*. Cambridge, MA: Harvard University Press.

Brooks, E., & Murray, J. 2018. Ready, Steady, Learn: School Readiness and Children's Voices in English Early Childhood Settings. *Education 3–13*, 46, 143–156.

Broström, S. 2017. A Dynamic Learning Concept in Early Years' Education: A Possible Way to Prevent Schoolification. *International Journal of Early Years Education*, 25, 3–15.

Brotherton, G., & Cronin, T. M. 2013. *Working with Vulnerable Children, Young People and Families*. London: Routledge.

Brown, K. 2017. *Vulnerability and Young People: Care and Social Control in Policy and Practice*. Bristol: Policy Press.

Brownlie, J., & Anderson, S. 2006. "Beyond Anti-Smacking": Rethinking Parent–Child Relations. *Childhood: A Global Journal of Child Research*, 13, 479–498.

Brummelman, E., Thomaes, S., Nelemans, S. A., de Castro, B. O., & Bushman, B. J. 2015. My Child Is God's Gift to Humanity: Development and Validation of the Parental Overvaluation Scale (POS). *Journal of Personality & Social Psychology*, 108, 665.

Brunsma, D. L., & Rockquemore, K. A. 2003. Statistics, Sound Bites, and School Uniforms: A Reply to Bodine. *The Journal of Educational Research*, 97, 72–77.

Bugler, T. 2018. Parents' Fears Stop Children Cycling or Walking to School. *The Times*.

Burman, C. J. 2018. The Taming Wicked Problems Framework: A Plausible Biosocial Contribution to 'Ending AIDS by 2030'. *The Journal for Transdisciplinary Research in Southern Africa*, 14, e1–e12.

Buzzelli, C. A. 2015. The Capabilities Approach: Rethinking Agency, Freedom, and Capital in Early Education. *Contemporary Issues in Early Childhood*, 16, 203–213.

Cameron, D. 2011. Troubled Families Speech. In: Cabinet Office (ed.). London.

Campbell-Barr, V., & Nygård, M. 2014. Losing Sight of the Child? Human Capital Theory and Its Role for Early Childhood Education and Care Policies in Finland and England Since the Mid-1990s. *Contemporary Issues in Early Childhood*, 15, 346–359.

Care Quality Commission. 2017. *The State of Health Care and Adult Social Care in England 2016/2017*. London.

Carver, A., Watson, B., Shaw, B., & Hillman, M. 2013. A Comparison Study of Children's Independent Mobility in England and Australia. *Childrens Geographies*, 11, 461–475.

Cassidy, C. 2012. Children's Status, Children's Rights and 'Dealing with' Children. *The International Journal of Children's Rights*, 20, 57–71.

Cavadel, E. W., & Frye, D. A. 2017. Not Just Numeracy and Literacy: Theory of Mind Development and School Readiness Among Low-Income Children. *Developmental Psychology*, 53, 2290.

Children's Commissioner. 2013. *A Child Rights Impact Assessment of the Anti-Social Behaviour, Crime and Policing Bill* (Parts 1–6, 9).

The Children's Society. 2018. *The Good Childhood Report 2018*. London.

Churchill, H. 2013. Retrenchment and Restructuring: Family Support and Children's Services Reform Under the Coalition. *Journal of Children's Services*, 8, 209–222. September.

Clapham, A. 2015. Producing the Docile Body: Analysing Local Area Under-Performance Inspection (LAUI). *Cambridge Journal of Education*, 45, 265–280.

Clow, D. 2013. An Overview of Learning Analytics. *Teaching in Higher Education*, 18, 683–695.
Cockcroft, T., Bryant, R., & Keval, H. 2016. The Impact of Dispersal Powers on Congregating Youth. *Safer Communities*, 15, 213–222.
Coe, R., Jones, K., Searle, J., Kokotsaki, D., Mohd Kosnin, A., & Skinner, P. 2008. *Evidence on the Effects of Selective Educational Systems*. Durham: CEM Centre and Durham University.
Cole, M. 1988. *Bowles and Gintis Revisited: Correspondence and Contradiction in Educational Theory.* London: Falmer Press.
Connely, K. 2018. Child Drownings in Germany Linked to Parents' Phone 'Fixation'. *The Guardian*.
Coram, & Coram, I. 2017. *Constructing a Definition of Vulnerability—Attempts to Define and Measure*. London.
Corby, F. H. 2015. Parenting Support: How Failing Parents Understand the Experience. *Journal of Education & Social Policy*, 2, 8.
Crawford, A. 2009. Criminalizing Sociability Through Anti-social Behaviour Legislation: Dispersal Powers, Young People and the Police. *Youth Justice*, 5, 5–26.
Crawford, A., & Lister, S. 2008. Young People, Police and Dispersal Powers. *Safer Communities*, 7, 4–7. April 1.
Crawford, S. B., Bennetts, S. K., Hackworth, N. J., Cooldin, A. R., Nicholson, J. M., Green, J., Graesser, H., Matthews, J., D'esposito, F., Strazdins, L., & Zubrick, S. R. 2017. Worries, 'Weirdos', Neighborhoods and Knowing People: A Qualitative Study with Children and Parents Regarding Children's Independent Mobility. *Health & Place*, 45, 131–139.
Creasy, R. 2018. *The Taming of Education*. Basingstoke: Palgrave Macmillan.
Cribbie, R. A. 2017. Multiplicity Control, School Uniforms, and Other Perplexing Debates. *Canadian Journal of Behavioural Science / Revue canadienne des sciences du comportement*, 49, 159.
Dahlberg, G. 2011. Policies in Early Childhood Education and Care: Potentialities for Agency, Play and Learning. In: Corsaro, W. A., Qvortrup, J., & Honig, M.-S. (eds.), *The Palgrave Handbook of Childhood Studies*. Basingstoke: Palgrave Macmillan.
Davey, C., & Lundy, L. 2011. Towards Greater Recognition of the Right to Play: An Analysis of Article 31 of the UNCRC. *Children and Society*, 25, 3–14.
Davies, W. 2014. *The Limits of Neoliberalism: Authority, Sovereignty and the Logic of Competition*. London: Sage.

De Magalhaes, C., & Trigo, S. F. 2017. Contracting Out Publicness: The Private Management of the Urban Public Realm and Its Implications. *Progress in Planning*, 115, 1–28.

Dean, M. 2014. Rethinking Neoliberalism. *Journal of Sociology*, 50, 13.

Deane, S. 2015. Dressing Diversity: Politics of Difference and the Case of School Uniforms. *Philosophical Studies in Education*, 46, 111–120.

Denzin, N. K., & Lincoln, Y. S. 2008. Introduction: The Discipline and Practice of Qualitative Research. In: Denzin, N. K., & Lincoln, Y. S. (eds.), *Strategies of Qualitative Enquiry*. 3rd ed. London: Sage.

DfE. 2017. Statutory Framework for the Early Years Foundation Stage: Setting the Standards for Learning, Development and Care for Children from Birth to Five. In: Education (ed.). London: HM Government.

DfES. 2004. *Every Child Matters: Change for Children/ Department for Education and Skills*. London: Department for Education and Skills.

Divers, A. 2017. Inculcating Agency. *Childhood & Philosophy*, 13, 253–270.

DoH. 2009. *Healthy Child Programme: Pregnancy and the First Five Years of Life*. London: Department of Health.

DoH. 2011. *Health Visitor Implementation Plan 2011–2015: A Call to Action*. London: Department of Health.

Donetto, S., & Maben, J. 2015. 'These Places Are Like a Godsend': A Qualitative Analysis of Parents' Experiences of Health Visiting Outside the Home and of Children's Centres Services. *Health Expectations*, 18, 2559–2569.

Dorn, S., & Ydesen, C. 2014. Towards a Comparative and International History of School Testing and Accountability. *Education Policy Analysis Archives*, 22, 1–11.

Dubiel, J., & Kilner, D. 2017. *Teaching Four and Five Year Olds: The Hundred Review of the Reception Year in England*. Available http://earlyexcellence.com/wp-content/uploads/2017/05/EX_TheHundredReview_ExecutiveSummary.pdf. Accessed 22 January 2018.

Ecclestone, K., & Hayes, D. 2009. *The Dangerous Rise of Therapeutic Education*. London: Routledge.

Ecclestone, K., & Lewis, L. 2014. Interventions for Resilience in Educational Settings: Challenging Policy Discourses of Risk and Vulnerability. *Journal of Education Policy*, 29, 195–216.

Evans, K. L. 2016. *Deconstructing 'Readiness' in Early Childhood Education*. University of Exeter.

Falchi, L., & Friedman, J. W. 2015. Rethinking the Discourse of Readiness in Preschool. In: Iorio, J. M., & Parnell, W. (eds.), *Rethinking Readiness in*

Early Childhood Education: Implications for Policy and Practice. New York, NY: Palgrave Macmillan.

Fattore, T., Mason, J., & Watson, E. 2007. Children's Conceptualisation(s) of Their Well-Being. *Social Indicators Research*, 80, 5–29.

Fava, N. M., Li, T., Burke, S. L., & Wagner, E. F. 2017. Resilience in the Context of Fragility: Development of a Multidimensional Measure of Child Wellbeing Within the Fragile Families Dataset. *Children and Youth Services Review*, 81, 358–367.

Fingerman, K. L., Cheng, Y.-P., Wesselmann, E. D., Zarit, S., Furstenberg, F., & Birditt, K. S. 2012. Helicopter Parents and Landing Pad Kids: Intense Parental Support of Grown Children. *Journal of Marriage & Family*, 74, 880–896.

Fletcher, D., & Sarkar, M. 2013. Psychological Resilience: A Review and Critique of Definitions, Concepts, and Theory. *European Psychologist*, 18, 12.

Foster, S., Villanueva, K., Wood, L., Christian, H., & Giles-Corti, B. 2014. The Impact of Parents' Fear of Strangers and Perceptions of Informal Social Control on Children's Independent Mobility. *Health & Place*, 26, 60–68.

Foucault, M. 1979. *Discipline and Punish: The Birth of the Prison*. Harmondsworth: Penguin.

Foucault, M. 1989. *The Archaeology of Knowledge*. London: Routledge.

Foundation, M. H. 2016. *Fundamental Facts About Mental Health 2016*. London: Mental Health Foundation.

Fox, C. 2016. *I Find That Offensive*. London: Biteback.

Foyster, E. 2013. The 'New World of Children' Reconsidered: Child Abduction in Late Eighteenth- and Early Nineteenth-Century England. *Journal of British Studies*, 52, 669–692.

Francis, J., Martin, K., Wood, L., & Foster, S. 2017. 'I'll Be Driving You to School for the Rest of Your Life': A Qualitative Study of Parents' Fear of Stranger Danger. *Journal of Environmental Psychology*, 53, 112–120.

Freeman, M., & Saunders, B. J. 2014. Can We Conquer Child Abuse If We Don't Outlaw Physical Chastisement of Children? *International Journal of Children's Rights*, 22, 681–709.

Frost, N., & Parton, N. 2009. *Understanding Children's Social Care: Politics, Policy and Practice*. Los Angeles: Sage.

Frydenberg, E. 2008. *Adolescent Coping: Advances in Theory, Research, and Practice*. London: Routledge.

Furedi, F. 2004. *Therapy Culture: Cultivating Vulnerability in an Uncertain Age*. London and New York: Routledge.

Furedi, F. 2008. *Paranoid Parenting: Why Ignoring the Experts May Be Best for Your Child.* London: Bloomsbury.

Gage, N. 2007. The Paradigm Wars and Their Aftermath: A 'Historical' Sketch of Research on Teaching Since 1989. In: Hammersley, M. (ed.), *Educational Research and Evidence-Based Practice.* London: Sage.

Gallagher, B. 2008. Fear of the Unknown. *Safer Communities*, 7, 22–25. July 1.

Garrett, P. M. 2009. *'Transforming' Children's Services? Social Work, Neoliberalism and the 'Modern' World.* Maidenhead, UK: Open University Press.

Garrett, P. B. 2018. *Welfare Words: Critical Social Work & Social Policy.* London: Sage.

George, M., & Odgers, C. 2015. Seven Fears and the Science of How Mobile Technologies May Be Influencing Adolescents in the Digital Age. *Perspectives on Psychological Science: A Journal of the Association for Psychological Science*, 10, 832–851.

Gibb, J., Jelicic, H., & La Valle, I. 2011. *Rolling Out Free Early Education for Disadvantaged Two Year Olds: An Implementation Study for Local Authorities and Providers.* London: National Children's Bureau.

Gill, T. 2007. *No Fear: Growing Up in a Risk Averse Society.* London: Calouste Gulbenkian Foundation.

Gillespie, J. 2013. Being and Becoming: Writing Children into Planning Theory. *Planning Theory*, 12, 64–80.

Gillis, J. 2009. Transitions to Modernity. In: Qvortrup, J., Corsaro, W. A., & Honig, M.-S. (eds.), *The Palgrave Handbook of Childhood Studies.* London: Palgrave.

Gronholm, P., Henderson, C., & Gronholm, P. C. 2018. Mental Health Related Stigma as a 'Wicked Problem': The Need to Address Stigma and Consider the Consequences. *International Journal of Environmental Research and Public Health*, 15, 1158.

Guldberg, H. 2009. *Reclaiming Childhood: Freedom and Play in an Age of Fear.* London: Routledge.

Gunderson, E. A., Gripshover, S. J., Romero, C., Dweck, C. S., Goldin-Meadow, S., & Levine, S. C. 2013. Parent Praise to 1- to 3-Year-Olds Predicts Children's Motivational Frameworks 5 Years Later. *Child Development*, 84, 1526–1541.

Gunderson, E. A., Sorhagen, N. S., Gripshover, S. J., Dweck, C. S., Goldin-Meadow, S., & Levine, S. C. 2018. Parent Praise to Toddlers Predicts

Fourth Grade Academic Achievement Via Children's Incremental Mindsets. *Developmental Psychology*, 54, 397.

Hackett, J. 2015. Top 10 Worst Health and Safety Myths. *Manager: British Journal of Administrative Management*, 2nd Quarter, 22–23, 2p.

Hall, J., Eisenstadt, N., Sylva, K., Smith, T., Sammons, P., Smith, G., Evangelou, M., Goff, J., Tanner, E., Agur, M., & Hussey, D. 2015. A Review of the Services Offered by English Sure Start Children's Centres in 2011 and 2012. *Oxford Review of Education*, 41, 89–104.

Hamilton-Giachritsis, C., Whittle, H., Beech, A., & Collings, G. 2013. A Review of Online Grooming: Characteristics and Concerns. *Aggression and Violent Behavior*, 18, 135–146.

Hamilton, W. 2011. Young People and Mental Health: Resilience and Models of Practice. In: O'Dell, L., & Leverett, S. (eds.), *Working with Children and Young People: Co-constructing Practice*. Basingstoke: Palgrave Macmillan.

Hammersley, M. (ed.). 2007. *Educational Research and Evidence-Based Practice*. London: Sage and The Open University.

Hanson, K. 2017. Embracing the Past: 'Been', 'Being' and 'Becoming' Children. *Childhood*, 24, 281–285.

Hardy, I. 2015. A Logic of Enumeration: The Nature and Effects of National Literacy and Numeracy Testing in Australia. *Journal of Education Policy*, 30, 335–362.

Hargreaves, A. 2003. *Teaching in the Knowledge Society: Education in the Age of Insecurity*. New York: Teachers College Press.

Harper, N. J. 2017. Outdoor Risky Play and Healthy Child Development in the Shadow of the "Risk Society": A Forest and Nature School Perspective. *Child & Youth Services*, 38, 318–334.

Harris, F. 2018. Outdoor Learning Spaces: The Case of Forest School. *Area*, 50, 222–231.

Hartog, J., & Oosterbeek, H. 2007. What Should You Know About the Private Returns to Education? In: Hartog, J., & Maassen Van Den Brink, H. (eds.), *Human Capital: Advances in Theory and Evidence*. Cambridge: Cambridge University Press.

Hasinoff, A. A. 2017. Where Are You? Location Tracking and the Promise of Child Safety. *Television & New Media*, 18, 496–512.

Hayden, C., & Jenkins, C. 2014. 'Troubled Families' Programme in England: 'Wicked Problems' and Policy-Based Evidence. *Policy Studies*, 35, 631–649.

Hegewisch, A., & Gornick, J. C. 2011. The Impact of Work-Family Policies on Women's Employment: A Review of Research from OECD Countries. *Community, Work & Family*, 14, 119–138.

Hendrick, H. 2005. Children and Social Policies. In: Hendrick, H. (ed.), *Child Welfare and Social Policy: An Essential Reader*. Bristol: Policy Press.

Heywood, C. 2018. *A History of Childhood*. Cambridge: Polity Press.

Horton, J., Christensen, P., Kraftl, P., & Hadfield-Hill, S. 2014. 'Walking … Just Walking': How Children and Young People's Everyday Pedestrian Practices Matter. *Social & Cultural Geography*, 15, 94–115.

Humphries, J. 2010. *Childhood and Child Labour in the British Industrial Revolution*. Cambridge, UK and New York: Cambridge University Press.

Hyndman, B. P., & Telford, A. 2015. Should Educators Be "Wrapping School Playgrounds in Cotton Wool" to Encourage Physical Activity? Exploring Primary and Secondary Students' Voices from the School Playground. *Australian Journal of Teacher Education*, 40, 4.

Van Ingen, D. J., Freiheit, S. R., Steinfeldt, J. A., Moore, L. L., Wimer, D. J., Knutt, A. D., Scapinello, S., & Roberts, A. 2015. Helicopter Parenting: The Effect of an Overbearing Caregiving Style on Peer Attachment and Self-Efficacy. *Journal of College Counseling*, 18, 7–20.

Iorio, J. M., & Parnell, W. 2015. *Rethinking Readiness in Early Childhood Education: Implications for Policy and Practice*. Basingstoke: Palgrave Macmillan.

James, A. 2009. Childhood Matters: Is Children's Wellbeing a High Enough Priority. *Mental Health Today*, 18.

James, A., & Prout, A. 1997. *Constructing and Reconstructing Childhood: Contemporary Issues in the Sociological Study of Childhood*. London: Falmer Press.

Jarram, M., & Pittam, D. 2017. *71 Students Put in Isolation for Wearing the Wrong Uniform on School's First Day of Term* (Online). Available http://www.nottinghampost.com/news/nottingham-news/71-students-put-isolation-wearing-437316. Accessed 12 January 2018.

Jenkins, N. E. 2006. 'You Can't Wrap Them Up in Cotton Wool!' Constructing Risk in Young People's Access to Outdoor Play. *Health, Risk & Society*, 8, 379–393.

Johnstone, C. 2016. After the Asbo: Extending Control Over Young People's Use of Public Space in England and Wales. *Critical Social Policy*, 36, 716–726.

Jordan, M. E., Kleinsasser, R. C., & Roe, M. F. 2014. Wicked Problems: Inescapable Wickedity. *Journal of Education for Teaching*, 40, 415–430.

Jupp, E. 2017. Families, Policy and Place in Times of Austerity. *Area*, 49, 266–272.

Kildare, C. A., & Middlemiss, W. 2017. Impact of Parents Mobile Device Use on Parent–Child Interaction: A Literature Review. *Computers in Human Behavior*, 75, 579–593.

Kish, A. M., & Newcombe, P. A. 2015. "Smacking Never Hurt Me!" Identifying Myths Surrounding the Use of Corporal Punishment. *Personality and Individual Differences*, 87, 121–129.

Knight, A., La Placa, V., & Mcnaught, A. (eds.). 2014. *Wellbeing: Policy and Practice*. Banbury: Lantern.

Knight, P., & Page, A. C. 2007. *The Assessment of 'Wicked' Competences*. Milton Keynes: Open University Practice-Based Professional Learning Centre.

Knight, S. 2009. *Forest Schools and Outdoor Learning in the Early Years*. Los Angeles, CA and London: Sage.

Knowles, G. 2009. *Ensuring Every Child Matters*. London and Thousand Oaks, CA: Sage.

Koshy, V., Pinheiro-Torres, C., & Portman-Smith, C. 2012. The Landscape of Gifted and Talented Education in England and Wales: How Are Teachers Implementing Policy? *Research Papers in Education*, 27, 167–186.

Kuhn, T. 1996. *The Structure of Scientific Revolutions*. Chicago: University of Chicago Press.

Lambie-Mumford, H., & Green, M. A. 2017. Austerity, Welfare Reform and the Rising Use of Food Banks by Children in England and Wales. *Area*, 49, 273–279.

Langston, A., & Abbott, L. 2004. *Birth to Three Matters: Supporting the Framework of Effective Practice*. Maidenhead: Open University Press.

Lavigueur, N. 2014. *The Wrong Trousers: Parents Angry After Pupils Put in Isolation at Colne Valley High School on First Day Back for 'Incorrect Trousers'* (Online). Available http://www.examiner.co.uk/news/west-yorkshire-news/wrong-trousers-parents-angry-after-7708277. Accessed 12 January 2018.

Layard, R. 2011. *Happiness: Lessons from a New Science*. London: Penguin.

Layard, R., & Dunn, J. 2009. *A Good Childhood: Searching for Values in a Competitive Age*. London: Penguin.

Lee, H. I., Kim, Y.-H., Kesebir, P., & Han, D. E. 2017. Understanding When Parental Praise Leads to Optimal Child Outcomes: Role of Perceived Praise Accuracy. *Social Psychological and Personality Science*, 8, 679–688.

Lemoyne, T., & Buchanan, T. 2011. Does 'Hovering' Matter? Helicopter Parenting and Its Effect on Well-Being. *Sociological Spectrum*, 31, 399–418.

Leverett, S. 2011. Children's Spaces. In: Foley, P., & Leverett, S. (eds.), *Children and Young Peoples Spaces: Developing Practice*. Basingstoke: Palgrave Macmillan.

Lewis, J. 2011. Parenting Programmes in England: Policy Development and Implementation Issues, 2005–2010. *Journal of Social Welfare & Family Law*, 33, 107–121.

Lewis, J., Cuthbert, R., & Sarre, S. 2011. What Are Children's Centres? The Development of CC Services, 2004–2008. *Social Policy & Administration*, 45, 35–53.

Lister, R. 2005. Investing in the Citizen-Workers of the Future. In: Hendrick, H. (ed.), *Child Welfare and Social Policy: An Essential Reader*. Bristol: Policy Press.

Lupton, D. 2016. *The Quantified Self*. Cambridge: Polity Press.

Lupton, D., & Williamson, B. 2017. The Datafied Child: The Dataveillance of Children and Implications for Their Rights. *New Media & Society*, 19, 780–794.

Lyon, C. M. 2007. Interrogating the Concentration on the UNCRC Instead of the ECHR in the Development of Children's Rights in England? *Children & Society*, 21, 147–153.

Macblain, S., Dunn, J., & Luke, I. 2017. *Contemporary Childhood*. London: Sage.

Macfarlane, B. 2017. *Freedom to Learn: The Threat to Student Academic Freedom and Why It Needs to Be Reclaimed*. Abingdon: Routledge.

Macfarlane, K., & Lakhani, A. 2015. Performativity, Propriety and Productivity: The Unintended Consequences of Investing in the Early Years. *Contemporary Issues in Early Childhood*, 16, 179–191.

Malone, K. 2007. The Bubble-Wrap Generation: Children Growing Up in Walled Gardens. *Environmental Education Research*, 13, 513–527.

Marano, H. E. 2004. A Nation of Wimps. *Psychology Today*, 37, 58–70.

Martínez-Martí, M. L., & Ruch, W. 2017. Character Strengths Predict Resilience Over and Above Positive Affect, Self-Efficacy, Optimism, Social Support, Self-Esteem, and Life Satisfaction. *The Journal of Positive Psychology*, 12, 110–119.

Mcnamee, S. 2016. *The Social Study of Childhood*. London: Palgrave.

Mcnaught, A. 2011. Defining Wellbeing. In: Knight, A., & Mcnaught, A. (eds.), *Understanding Wellbeing: An Introduction for Students and Practitioners of Health and Social Care*. New York: Lantern Publishing.

Michaela. 2018. *RE: Michaela Behaviour Policy*.

Miller, L., & Hevey, D. 2012. *Policy Issues in the Early Years*. Thousand Oaks, CA and London: Sage.

Mirowski, P. 2014. *The Political Movement That Dared Not Speak Its Own Name: The Neoliberal Thought Collective Under Erasure*. Available https://www.ineteconomics.org/uploads/papers/WP23-Mirowski.pdf. Accessed 11 October 2016.

Mirowski, P., & Plehwe, D. (eds.). 2009. *The Road from Mont Pèlerin: The Making of the Neoliberal Thought Collective*. Cambridge, MA: Harvard University Press.

Morrissey, T. W., & Vinopal, K. 2018. Center-Based Early Care and Education and Children's School Readiness: Do Impacts Vary by Neighborhood Poverty? *Developmental Psychology*, 54, 757–771.

Moss, P., Dillon, J., & Statham, J. 2000. The 'Child in Need' and 'the Rich Child': Discourses, Constructions and Practice. *Critical Social Policy*, 20, 233–254.

Mulryan-Kyne, C. 2014. The School Playground Experience: Opportunities and Challenges for Children and School Staff. *Educational Studies*, 40, 377–395.

Murray, J. 2017. Young Children Are Human Beings. *International Journal of Early Years Education*, 25, 1–2.

Neaum, S. 2016. School Readiness and Pedagogies of Competence and Performance: Theorising the Troubled Relationship Between Early Years and Early Years Policy. *International Journal of Early Years Education*, 24, 239–253.

NESS. 2012. *The Impact of Sure Start Local Programmes on Seven Year Olds and Their Families London: Institute for the Study of Children, Families and Social Issues*. Birkbeck: University of London.

OECD. 2009. *Doing Better for Children*. Paris: OECD.

Ofsted. 2014. *Below the Radar: Low-Level Disruption in the Country's Classrooms*. London: Ofsted.

Ofsted. 2017. Bold Beginnings: The Reception Curriculum in a Sample of Good and Outstanding Primary Schools. In: Ofsted (ed.). Manchester.

Ofsted, & Spielman, A. 2017. *Amanda Spielman's Speech at the ASCL Annual Conference* (Online). HM Government. Available https://www.gov.uk/government/speeches/amanda-spielmans-speech-at-the-ascl-annual-conference. Accessed 24 March 2017.

Ofsted, & Spielman, A. 2018. *Amanda Spielman Speech to the Schools NorthEast Summit* (Online). London: Ofsted. Available https://www.gov.

uk/government/speeches/amanda-spielman-speech-to-the-schools-north-east-summit. Accessed 18 October 2018.

Olsson, C. A., Bond, L., Burns, J. M., Vella-Brodrick, D. A., & Sawyer, S. M. 2003. Adolescent Resilience: A Concept Analysis. *Journal of Adolescence*, 26, 1–11.

ONS. 2018. *Statistical Bulletin: UK Labour Market: February 2018 Estimates of Employment, Unemployment, Economic Inactivity and Other Employment-Related Statistics for the UK*. London: Office for National Statistics.

Padilla-Walker, L. M., & Nelson, L. J. 2012. Black Hawk Down? Establishing Helicopter Parenting as a Distinct Construct from Other Forms of Parental Control During Emerging Adulthood. *Journal of Adolescence*, 35, 1177–1190.

Pain, R. 2006. Paranoid Parenting? Rematerializing Risk and Fear for Children. *Social & Cultural Geography*, 7, 221–243.

Palmer, S. 2007. *Detoxing Childhood: What Parents Need to Know to Raise Happy, Successful Children*. London: Orion.

Palmer, S. 2009. What Is Toxic Childhood. In: House, R., & Loewenthal, D. (eds.), *Childhood, Well-Being, and a Therapeutic Ethos*. London: Karnac Books.

Palmer, S. 2015. *Toxic Childhood: How the Modern World Is Damaging Our Children and What We Can Do About It*. London: Orion Books.

Peluchette, J. V. E., Kovanic, N., & Partridge, D. 2013. Helicopter Parents Hovering in the Workplace: What Should HR Managers Do? *Business Horizons*, 56, 601–609.

Perry, N. B., Dollar, J. M., Calkins, S. D., Keane, S. P., & Shanahan, L. 2018. Childhood Self-Regulation as a Mechanism Through Which Early Overcontrolling Parenting Is Associated with Adjustment in Preadolescence. *Developmental Psychology*, 54, 1542–1555.

Phillips, J. 2017. *Pupils Banned from Cheltenham Bournside School for Wearing Wrong Trousers* (Online). Available http://www.gloucestershirelive.co.uk/news/cheltenham-news/pupils-banned-cheltenham-bournside-school-432153. Accessed 12 January 2017.

Pike, J. 2008. Foucault, Space and Primary School Dining Rooms. *Children's Geographies*, 6, 413–422.

Pike, J., & Kelly, P. 2014. *The Moral Geographies of Children, Young People and Food: Beyond Jamie's School Dinners*. Basingstoke: Palgrave Macmillan.

Plowright, D. 2011. *Using Mixed Methods: Frameworks for an Integrated Methodology*. London: Sage.

Postman, N. 1994. *The Disappearance of Childhood*. New York: Vintage.

References

Preece, A. 2018. 'Prison-Like' School Tells Pupils to Walk Between Classes in Silence at Ninestiles, an Academy. *Birmingham Live*.

Pring, R. 2004. *Philosophy of Education: Aims, Theory, Common Sense and Research*. London: Continuum.

Qvortrup, J., Honig, M.-S., & Corsaro, W. A. 2009. *The Palgrave Handbook of Childhood Studies*. Basingstoke, NY: Palgrave Macmillan.

Radesky, J., Miller, A. L., Rosenblum, K. L., Appugliese, D., Kaciroti, N., & Lumeng, J. C. 2015. Maternal Mobile Device Use During a Structured Parent–Child Interaction Task. *Academic Pediatrics*, 15, 238–244.

Radnor, H., Koshy, V., & Taylor, A. 2007. Gifts, Talents and Meritocracy. *Journal of Education Policy*, 22, 283–299.

Ravitch, D. 1998. What If Research Really Mattered? *Education Week*, 18, 33.

Richards, C. 2012. Playing Under Surveillance: Gender, Performance and the Conduct of the Self in a Primary School Playground. *British Journal of Sociology of Education*, 33, 373–390.

Rittel, H. W. J., & Webber, M. M. 1973. Dilemmas in a General Theory of Planning. *Policy Sciences*, 4, 155–169.

Roberts-Holmes, G. 2015. The 'Datafication' of Early Years Pedagogy: 'If the Teaching Is Good, the Data Should Be Good and If There's Bad Teaching, There Is Bad Data'. *Journal of Education Policy*, 30, 302–315.

Roberts-Holmes, G., & Bradbury, A. 2016. Governance, Accountability and the Datafication of Early Years Education in England. *British Educational Research Journal*, 42, 600–613.

Roberts, R. 2010. *Wellbeing from Birth*. London: Sage.

Romagnoli, A., & Wall, G. 2012. 'I Know I'm a Good Mom': Young, Low-Income Mothers' Experiences with Risk Perception, Intensive Parenting Ideology and Parenting Education Programmes. *Health, Risk & Society*, 14, 273–289.

Rönkä, A., Malinen, K., Metsäpelto, R.-L., Laakso, M.-L., Sevón, E., & Verhoef-Van Dorp, M. 2017. Parental Working Time Patterns and Children's Socioemotional Wellbeing: Comparing Working Parents in Finland, the United Kingdom, and the Netherlands. *Children and Youth Services Review*, 76, 133–141.

Van Rosmalen, L., Van der Horst, F. C. P., & Van der Veer, R. 2016. From Secure Dependency to Attachment: Mary Ainsworth's Integration of Blatz's Security Theory into Bowlby's Attachment Theory. *History of Psychology*, 19, 22.

Van Rosmalen, L., Van der Veer, R., & Van der Horst, F. 2015. Ainsworth's Strange Situation Procedure: The Origin of an Instrument. *Journal of the History of the Behavioral Sciences*, 51, 261–284.

Russell, J. S. 2015. Resilience. *Journal of the Philosophy of Sport*, 42, 159–183.
Sayer, T. 2008. *Critical Practice in Working with Children.* Basingstoke, NY: Palgrave Macmillan.
Schiffrin, H., Godfrey, H., Liss, M., & Erchull, M. 2015. Intensive Parenting: Does It Have the Desired Impact on Child Outcomes? *Journal of Child & Family Studies*, 24, 2322–2331.
Schouten, L. 2015. Ban on 'Tag': Are School Children Getting the Right Playtime? *Christian Science Monitor.*
Sharma-Stray, L., & Creasy, R. 2013. Children as Playtime Monitors: What It Means for the Monitor. *Pastoral Care in Education*, 31, 229–239.
Shaw, B., Watson, B., Frauendienst, B., Redecker, A., Jones, T., & Hillman, M. 2013. *Children's Independent Mobility: A Comparative Study in England and Germany (1971–2010).* London: Policy Studies Institute.
Simpson, B. 2014. Tracking Children, Constructing Fear: GPS and the Manufacture of Family Safety. *Information and Communications Technology Law*, 23, 273–285.
Simpson, D., & Envy, R. 2015. Subsidizing Early Childhood Education and Care for Parents on Low Income: Moving Beyond the Individualized Economic Rationale of Neoliberalism. *Contemporary Issues in Early Childhood*, 16, 166–178.
Sixsmith, J., Gabhainn, S. N., Fleming, C., & O'Higgins, S. 2007. Children's, Parents' and Teachers' Perceptions of Child Wellbeing. *Health Education*, 107, 511–523.
Smith, F. 2013. Parents and Policy Under New Labour: A Case Study of the United Kingdom's New Deal for Lone Parents. *Children's Geographies*, 11, 160–172.
Smith, K. M. 2014. *The Government of Childhood: Discourse, Power and Subjectivity.* Basingstoke: Palgrave Macmillan.
Sointu, E. 2005. The Rise of an Ideal: Tracing Changing Discourses of Wellbeing. *Sociological Review*, 53, 255–274.
Spratt, J. 2016. Childhood Wellbeing: What Role for Education? *British Educational Research Journal*, 42, 223–239.
Star, T. 2009. *Children Sent Home from School for Wearing Wrong Trousers* (Online). Sheffield. Available https://www.thestar.co.uk/whats-on/out-and-about/children-sent-home-from-school-for-wearing-wrong-trousers-1-297085. Accessed 12 January 2018.
Stearns, P. N. 2003. *Anxious Parents: A History of Modern Childrearing in America.* New York: New York University Press.

Stephenson, K. 2016. *"It's Not for the Sake of a Ribboned Coat": A History of British School Uniform.* University of York.

Stern, J. 2014. *Loneliness and Solitude in Education: How to Value Individuality and Create an Enstatic School.* Oxford and New York: Peter Lang.

Stevens, I., & Hassett, P. 2007. Applying Complexity Theory to Risk in Child Protection Practice. *Childhood: A Global Journal of Child Research*, 14, 128–144.

Stevenson, H. 2017. The "Datafication" of Teaching: Can Teachers Speak Back to the Numbers? *Peabody Journal of Education*, 92, 537–557. https://doi.org/10.1080/0161956X.2017.1349492.

Stewart, W. 2006. New Register for the Gifted and Talented. *TES: Times Educational Supplement.*

Stirrup, J., Evans, J., & Davies, B. 2017a. Early Years Learning, Play Pedagogy and Social Class. *British Journal of Sociology of Education*, 38, 872–886.

Stirrup, J., Evans, J., & Davies, B. 2017b. Learning One's Place and Position Through Play: Social Class and Educational Opportunity in Early Years Education. *International Journal of Early Years Education*, 25, 343–360.

Storr, W. 2017. *Selfie: How We Became So Self-Obsessed and What It's Doing to Us.* London: Picador.

Strelitz, J. 2013. "It Sounds Good But…": Children's Centre Managers' Views of Evidence-Based Practice. *Journal of Children's Services*, 8, 21–30. March 15.

Suissa, J. 2013. Tiger Mothers and Praise Junkies: Children, Praise and the Reactive Attitudes. *Journal of Philosophy of Education*, 47, 1–19.

Sundhall, J. 2017. A Political Space for Children? The Age Order and Children's Right to Participation. *Social Inclusion*, 5, 164–171.

Sutterby, J. A. 2009. What Kids Don't Get to Do Anymore and Why. *Childhood Education*, 85, 289–292.

TACTYC. 2017. *Bald Beginnings* (Online). Association for Professional Development in Early Years. Available http://tactyc.org.uk/wp-content/uploads/2017/12/Bold-Beginnings-TACTYC-response-FINAL-09.12.17.pdf. Accessed 22 January 2018.

Taket, A. R., Nolan, A., & Stagnitti, K. 2014. Family Strategies to Support and Develop Resilience in Early Childhood. *Early Years: An International Journal of Research and Development*, 34, 289–300.

Taylor, D. 2011. Wellbeing and Welfare: A Psychosocial Analysis of Being Well and Doing Well Enough. *Journal of Social Policy*, 40, 777–794.

Taylor, Z. E., Eisenberg, N., Spinrad, T. L., & Widaman, K. F. 2013. Longitudinal Relations of Intrusive Parenting and Effortful Control to Ego-Resiliency During Early Childhood. *Child Development*, 84, 1145–1151.

Telegraph. 2018. Pupils Banned from Talking While Walking Between Lessons Under Headteacher's Silence Policy. *Daily Telegraph*.

Thomson, S. 2003. A Well-Equipped Hamster Cage: The Rationalisation of Primary School Playtime. *Education 3–13*, 31, 54–59.

Thomson, S. 2007. Do's and Don'ts: Children's Experiences of the Primary School Playground. *Environmental Education Research*, 13, 487–500.

Times. 2017. Snowflake Generation Seek Solace in Safe Spaces. *The Times*.

Tobin, J., Hsueh, Y., & Karasawa, M. 2011. *Preschool in Three Cultures Revisited: China, Japan, and the United States*. Chicago, IL: University of Chicago Press.

Tovey, H. 2007. *Playing Outdoors: Spaces and Places, Risk and Challenge*. Maidenhead: McGraw-Hill and Open University Press.

Truelove, S. 2018. Croydon School Bans Pupils from Talking in Corridors and Says It Has Transformed Behaviour. *Croydon Advertiser*.

Tunstill, J., & Willow, C. 2017. Professional Social Work and the Defence of Children's and Their Families' Rights in a Period of Austerity: A Case Study. *Social Work & Social Sciences Review*, 19, 40–65.

Turnbull, G. 2016. The Price of Youth: Commodification of Young People Through Malleable Risk Practices. *Journal of Youth Studies*, 19, 1007–1021.

Turnbull, G., & Spence, J. 2011. What's at Risk? The Proliferation of Risk Across Child and Youth Policy in England. *Journal of Youth Studies*, 14, 939–959.

Turner, R. S. 2011. *Neo-Liberal Ideology: History, Concepts and Policies*. Edinburgh: Edinburgh University Press.

Underdown, A., & Barlow, J. 2012. Promoting Infant Mental Health: A Public Health Priority and Approach. In: Miller, L. & Hevey, D. (eds.), *Policy Issues in the Early Years*. London: Sage.

UNICEF. 1989. *UN Convention of the Rights of the Child* (Online). UNICEF. Available https://www.unicef.org/rightsite/237.htm. Accessed 12 March 2018.

Uprichard, E. 2008. Children as 'Being and Becomings': Children, Childhood and Temporality. *Children & Society*, 22, 303–313.

Veltkamp, G., & Brown, P. 2017. The Everyday Risk Work of Dutch Child-Healthcare Professionals: Inferring 'Safe' and 'Good' Parenting Through Trust, as Mediated by a Lens of Gender and Class. *Sociology of Health & Illness*, 39, 1297–1313.

Vincent, C. 2017. "The Children Have Only Got One Education and You Have to Make Sure It's a Good One": Parenting and Parent–School Relations in a Neoliberal Age. *Gender and Education*, 29, 541–557.

Vincent, C., & Maxwell, C. 2016. Parenting Priorities and Pressures: Furthering Understanding of 'Concerted Cultivation'. *Discourse: Studies in the Cultural Politics of Education*, 37, 269–281.

Vincent, C. D., & Neis, B. L. 2011. Work and Family Life: Parental Work Schedules and Child Academic Achievement. *Community, Work & Family*, 14, 449–468.

Vota, N. 2017. Keeping the Free-Range Parent Immune from Child Neglect: You Cannot Tell Me How to Raise My Children. *Family Court Review*, 55, 152–167.

Walkerdine, V. 2009. Developmental Psychology and the Study of Childhood. In: Kehily, M. J. (ed.), *An Introduction to Childhood*. 2nd ed. Maidenhead: Open University Press.

Wall, J. 2008. Human Rights in Light of Childhood. *International Journal of Children's Rights*, 16, 523–543.

Warnock, M. 2004. *Making Babies: Is There a Right to Have Children?* Oxford: Oxford University Press.

Wellard, I., & Secker, M. 2017. 'Visions' for Children's Health and Wellbeing: Exploring the Complex and Arbitrary Processes of Putting Theory into Practice. *Sport, Education and Society*, 22, 586–601.

Wells, K. 2018. *Childhood Studies*. Cambridge: Polity Press.

West, A., & Noden, P. 2016. Public Funding of Early Years Education in England: An Historical Perspective. *Clare Market Papers*, 21.

Wexler, M. 2009. Exploring the Moral Dimension of Wicked Problems. *International Journal of Sociology and Social Policy*, 29, 531–542.

Wheway, R. 2008. *Not a Risk Averse Society: Fair Play for Children*. 2nd ed. Bognor Regis: Fair Play for Children.

Whittle, H., Hamilton-Giachritsis, C., Beech, A., & Collings, G. 2013. A Review of Young People's Vulnerabilities to Online Grooming. *Aggression and Violent Behavior*, 18, 135–146.

Wilkes, S. 2011. *The Children History Forgot*. London: Robert Hale.

Wilkinson, R., & Pickett, K. 2018. *The Inner Level: How More Equal Societies Reduce Stress, Restore Sanity and Improve Everyone's Wellbeing*. London: Allen Lane.

Wilkinson, R. G., & Pickett, K. 2010. *The Spirit Level: Why Equality Is Better for Everyone*. London: Penguin.

Williams, F. 2004. *Rethinking Families*. London: Calouste Gulbenkian Foundation.

Wilson, A., Watson, C., Thompson, T. L., Drew, V., & Doyle, S. 2017. Learning Analytics: Challenges and Limitations. *Teaching in Higher Education*, 22, 991–1007.

Wright, N. 2011. Between 'Bastard' and 'Wicked' Leadership? School Leadership and the Emerging Policies of the UK Coalition Government. *Journal of Educational Administration and History*, 43, 17.

Wrigley, T. 2009. Rethinking Education in the Era of Globalization. In: Hill, D. (ed.), *Contesting Neo-Liberal Education: Public Resistance and Collective Advance*. Abingdon: Routledge.

Wyness, M. G. 2012. *Childhood and Society*. Basingstoke: Palgrave Macmillan.

Zhang, X. 2017. Identifying Consumerist Privately Owned Public Spaces: The Ideal Type of Mass Private Property. *Urban Studies*, 54, 3464–3479.

Index

A
Accountability 109
Austerity 24

B
Bold Beginnings 90
Bronfenbrenner, U. 89, 127

C
Child
  labour 20, 72, 90
  mortality 72
Childhood
  government of 88
  as middle-class 90
  as process 37, 38, 104, 108
  as project 66
Children
  as becomings 6, 17, 18, 88, 104
  as beings 6, 17, 19, 104, 134
  bubble-wrapped, cotton-wool 70
  discipline 64, 115
  as emotional investment 71, 72
  poverty 24, 25, 59
  proper place/location 62, 74, 75
  as threat 63
  as unique 43
  as valued 96
Children's centres 89, 92
conditions of possibility 52

D
Data 110
  datafication 110, 112, 113
  data points 111
  learning analytics 112, 113
Developmental psychology 19

Index

E
Early intervention 59
Early Years
　Foundation stage 84, 91
　Professional Status 84
Education 104, 108, 119
　outcomes 66, 131
Emotions 73
Every Child Matters (ECM) 9, 88, 94
Evidence-based practice 44, 46

F
Families 87
　troubled families 59
Forest schools 96

H
Health Visitors/Visiting 85
　and surveillance 86
Home 61
Human Capital 6, 118

I
Individualisation/individualism 16
Inequality 24

L
Learning 108
Learning analytics 112
Life choices 16

M
Mental health 2, 24, 36, 128
Metrics 111
Milestones 19
Mobile phones 61, 73
　Phone apps 69
Multi-agency working 46

N
Neoliberalism 14, 15, 23, 29, 113

O
Ofsted 3, 90, 109, 120

P
Paradigms 44, 68
Parents/Parenting 3, 44, 58, 59, 85
　'Good' parents 4, 62, 63, 71, 129
　hard to reach 126
　helicopter parents 8, 23, 64, 65, 67, 129
　involvement 65
　paranoid 129
　policies 60
　responsibilities 63
Play 18, 61, 63, 85, 91, 97, 107
Playgrounds 106
Potential 19, 73, 104
Power 58, 62, 117
Pubs 75

R

Readiness 88, 92, 93, 108
Resilience 3, 4, 27, 44, 132
Rights 18, 21, 63, 73, 119, 127
Risk 25, 39, 58, 71, 74, 95
   risk averse 39
Rittel, J 2, 4, 14, 36, 133

S

Safeguarding 65, 94
Schools
   Grammar schools 130
   quiet corridors 105
   readiness 108
   schoolification 108
   schooling 63
School uniform 114–118
   types 116
Self-esteem 40
Snowflakes 7, 36, 38, 41, 44
Social class 92, 104
Socialisation 5
Solitude 64
Space 61, 63, 69
State 84, 86, 88
Surveillance 68, 69, 74

T

Tame 17, 37, 50
   tameness 5, 14, 36–43, 132
   taming 41, 75, 117
   town planning 20

U

United Nations Convention on the Rights of the Child (UNCRC) 4, 18, 52, 134

V

Values 43, 116
Vulnerability 6, 25–27, 94

W

Webber, M. 2, 4, 14, 36, 133
Wellbeing/wellbecoming 2, 4, 21–24, 128
Wicked 37
   in education 45
   and risk 51
   wicked problems 49
Work 19, 71, 72, 86, 87, 97, 116, 117